PREDATOR TRAINING

ASHLEY,
Keep UP The Great Training.
Dave Hopkins

* Ashley — Train Hard!

•   •   •   •   •   •   •

This book is dedicated to the people I've known who have reached deep within themselves to find their personal best and shared their treasure of excellence generously, and then *inspired* me to find that place within myself.

That the world at large outside the martial art community has never heard of them doesn't alter the fact that these people are legendary. Legends, because in a world where we can live life large, they became giants! Giants, because they had the inner ferocity to go after what they wanted out of life rather than being content to be spoon-fed.

Two such men who have raised and mastered the beast are Grandmaster Jimmy H. Woo and Master Al Rubin. These two have gone on to a greater challenge and leave behind the legacy of generations of people who've been taught to open their eyes and their minds to see and live the lives most can only dream of.

PREDATOR

THE INNER BEAST OF SAN SOO

TRAINING

MASTER GREG JONES

PALADIN PRESS
BOULDER, COLORADO

Also by Master Greg Jones:

Sudden Violence: The Art of San Soo

Predator Training: The Inner Beast of San Soo
by Master Greg Jones

Copyright © 1993 by Greg Jones

ISBN 0-87364-724-6
Printed in the United States of America

Published by Paladin Press, a division of
Paladin Enterprises, Inc., P.O. Box 1307,
Boulder, Colorado 80306, USA.
(303) 443-7250

Direct inquiries and/or orders to the above address.

Photographs by Loveall/Smith Photography

CONTENTS

This book wouldn't be written and shared were it not for the encouragement and persistence of Jon Ford, editor at Paladin Press. I told him the *possibility of the manuscript,* and he believed in the *reality of the book.* At times when I'd stray from the word processor long enough to lose momentum in this project to pursue some adventure I'd invariably end up healing from, I'd hear from Jon and he'd give me a gentle prod back in the direction of this book. And now that it's finished, I'd like to send him a jug of whiskey and a friendly blonde of obscene proportions (but my wife won't let me). Thanks, Jon.

I want to thank those people who were supportive of this project but didn't appear within these pages: My great friend Bruce Fountain, who lent his support and encouragement, who was featured throughout my first book, and who had a long-standing commitment to helping me by modeling for photos in this one. Unfortunately, I'd procrastinated too long and ran up against a deadline that found my friend and me on opposite ends of the rainbow. Sorry, Bruce.

Shihan Peter Browne and Sensei David Singh of the United Kingdom Kempo Jiu Jitsu Association had modeled for some early photo sequences at London's Heathrow Airport. Unfortunately, my lack of photographic skills prevented me from sharing with you some dynamic action scenes with them. I'd been graciously invited to England to demonstrate the art of kung fu san soo at the K.J.J.A. Annual Self-Defense Seminar and was accorded a wonderful opportunity to share knowledge

ACKNOWLEDGMENTS

with some very knowledgeable new friends who really know the meaning of hospitality. Thanks, Peter; thanks, David.

I'd like also to acknowledge and thank my wife of 24 years for her encouragement and support of me, my projects, and my misadventures through these many years (thanks, Cheryl). And I want to express my appreciation of my sons, Greg and Chris, for their headlong dedication to their study of san soo, for not complaining about my beating the crap out of them during their training with me, and for enduring the rigors of being on the receiving end of my demos. I'd be remiss if I didn't take further advantage of this space to make a public statement of the fact that, beyond this and anything else I'm ever able to accomplish in this lifetime, my sons have made me more proud than any man could possibly have a right to be. Thanks, Greg; thanks, Chris.

I'm also happy to include my son's lovely wife, Vicky, in some photos. Thanks, Vicky. You're a wonderful daughter and a terrific life-support system for my grandchild!

I'm happy to again have my radiant friend, Casey Dale, participate in the photo shoot. Casey and his also radiant wife, Chrissy, have been instrumental in revitalizing my interest in writing. I've found that inspiration can be a gift more precious than gold. Thanks, Casey; thanks, Chrissy.

I'd also like to mention my gratitude for the friendship and cooperation of Tim McMahen. Tim is a skydiving free-fall cameraman who came to my rescue when a parachute/bungee adventure went to hell in a heartbeat. Tim took the time off from his work to help me get the photographs for this book. Unfortunately, the times and circumstances, particularly the Oregon weather in which we took photos, proved too big an obstacle in too short notice. Otherwise, the entire book would have been photographed by Tim McMahen. Thanks, Tim.

I'd like to thank my brother-in-law, Roger Tapiceria, for the cover photo of this book, and I apologize for neglecting to mention his photos in my last one. Thanks, Roger. I'd also like to thank my friend and fellow san soo practitioner Bob Shores for enduring the cover photo shoot while I crunched his throat to get just the right look. Thanks, Bob.

Finally, I'd like to thank photographer David Loveall of Loveall/Smith Photography for orchestrating, supervising, and giving priority to getting the photographs finished on time in his studio. Thanks, David. Steve Smith took the photos for the book and did an exceptional job of making a difficult shoot run smoothly. Thanks, Steve. Cliff Etzel worked long, continuous hours developing the B&W prints for this book. The fumes must have been awful, and yet, perhaps that's the reason he found my jokes so funny. Thanks, Cliff.

Our lives follow more routine patterns than we might believe. And the biggest danger in a routine is that it is, by definition, predictable—we usually think the usual things will usually happen at the usual time, place, and condition. Today, however, will be quite different from your usual routine.

Today you will leave work at your usual time. Your leaving the workplace is consistent with your normal routine. You're tired and preoccupied with the day's events. What lies in store for you around the corner is far from routine; it will be a crossroad, a turning point, a point of no return where you will have to set aside your personal ethic about the sanctity of life in order to survive.

You will have to call up from within you a primal and predatory beast that lurks in the shadows of your civilized psyche. You're aware of its existence, despite the number of times you've denied it room to prowl and the opportunity to grow. In the next few moments, you will *become* either predator or prey.

But wait! That's too easy. We both know you'd be a goner in seconds with what you're about to walk into. Let's say instead that you were aware of the beast, and you gave it every opportunity to grow and prowl. You and the beast within are close buddies. This facet of your primal self awaits just such an opportunity to breathe life into itself, in order to protect you, that it might continue to live. The beast is your survival instinct!

This page begins to look wavy and dreamlike as we gaze into a crystal-ball image of a possible future. (Of course your job will still suck, but then, so will mine.)

And as he stands there, casually flicking

a Filipino butterfly knife back and forth, smiling at his friends who begin to flank you as you approach your parked car, he makes the most costly error of his entire life . . . *he underestimates you!*

Your post-work tiredness and preoccupation are gone. You are now radiantly alive and alert, processing every sound and flicker of light. Your sense of smell is heightened to a degree that you can detect the stench of unwashed clothes and bodies outside your peripheral vision. The predator within has been awakened; the people are now prey, and prey is always *meat!*

As the others begin to close in on you, and you know for certain you're going to be attacked, you stalk within striking range of the one with the knife. He's the apparent leader of this little group, and he's also your nearest prey.

When he begins to speak to you, his eyes widen in shock as you plunge into the middle of him and in one fluid movement pull him in tight as you stab your right thumb deep into his eye socket, with the fingers sliding in and clutching his hair tightly in your fist. You then pivot into him and slam the palm of your other hand into his chin as you pull his head to you, effectively breaking his neck to take his life while rotating his body between you and the other members of his group.

This was done so smoothly and quickly, the horror and finality of what you've done just now begins to register with them. The one nearest you and your victim sees the copious blood flow and viscous fluid trailing down his leader's face and your hand. He also exhibits the accompanying shock of

witnessing his friend's death at your hands
and becomes immediately indecisive as to
what to do now. He experiences shock,
rage, fear, confusion, and then sheer panic
as he recognizes the fact that *he's next!* He
and his little company watch in disbelief as
you let your prey crumple at your feet and
begin to calmly but intently stalk toward
them. You are cold, detached, and intensely
focused upon the prey around you. They
scatter in every direction without ever
understanding why. *You know why,* and
that's all that matters.

• • • • • • •

As you become acquainted with the art
of kung fu san soo through the following
pages, you may find that you're also
becoming more acquainted with yourself in
the process. You may discover at the
completion of this book that you've been
put in touch with a predator within yourself
that's been as much a part of you as your
own shadow.

Whatever you discover about yourself,
whether you deem it good or bad won't
really matter. We tend to make value
judgments about practically everything, and
that's alright because it's simply human
nature. Ultimately, you'll learn that it's
perfect to simply BE, without feeling guilty
or ashamed of what you're capable of and
how much pain or injury you can inflict.
Whether you can or can't hurt someone or
take an attacker's life won't have any
bearing on whether you're a "good" or a
"bad" person. You will simply do *what must
be done* and then get on with your life.

Before plunging headlong into the actual techniques and applications of Fut Ga, the most violent application of the art of san soo, I'm going to share with you a philosophy of sorts that you may feel free to dismiss or adhere to as you will. It won't make any difference at all in the application of this art.

At the dawn of mankind, before there was ever a spoken language, when there was little distinction between man and beast, it was a natural state to be both predator and prey. When we hunted animals for food and fought off other humans from encroaching on what we deemed our sanctuary/territory, we were predator. When we discovered that the animals were much better adapted to hunting us, we became prey.

Being both predator and prey is a fact of life even still, regardless of how civilized we believe ourselves to be. Do you doubt this? Travel (if you dare) down the back alleys and skid rows of any metropolitan area and look at its inhabitants in the Stygian darkness they feel most at home in. And just for fun, so you can get them interested enough in you for a closer look, leave some money peeking out of every pocket and try to act nervous.

Well now, it seems you don't have long to wait after all. Look over there at the edge of that old hotel next to the alley, the one with the wino urinating on the sidewalk (mostly on his shoes). See the guy next to him? Yeah that's the one; he's got long, scraggly hair wrapped in a bandana, tattoos, denim vest, dirty clothes, and scars on his bare arms and down one cheek. And look, he's keeping pace with you across the street. He hasn't taken his eyes off you for a second.

Keep walking at the same stride, and look directly ahead of you down the sidewalk. About 50 yards in front of you, there are two more people that are taking an interest in you. They're equally grubby and are perched on either side of the sidewalk. What are you slowing down for? C'mon, let's go meet them; after all, they do seem to like you. Look at the way they smile at you!

There's been a subtle signal given and acknowledged, and as they begin to converge on you, notice the feral look in their eyes. (The only real difference between them and animals is that your newfound "friends'" eyes don't glow in the dark.) Hmmm, imagine that; the closer you get to them, the more interested they become. They must really like you!

Looks like the romance is over. They're looking pretty intense as they close in on you. Well, I gotta go now, but be sure and tell them that you aren't really prey. I'm sure they'll understand.

• • • • • • •

In order to make a behavioral modification in yourself to be able to assimilate predatory traits and skills, you must first begin by at least becoming assertive. Are you now assertive?

When someone cuts in front of you while you're standing in line, do you say anything?

When someone stares at you, do you look away or take issue with it?

When someone rudely bumps into you, do you apologize or tell him to watch where he's going?

This list can continue into many areas. The point to be made is that to begin to be a predator, *you have to begin by being assertive!* Assertion doesn't mean rudeness; it is simply an affirmation of your inherent right not to be treated badly but with "respect." The same respect you offer others is what you can expect and command for yourself.

Remember this: you aren't actually learning to become a predator any more than you're learning to become a human, because each is your natural state of being. Through the centuries, civilization has taken its toll on our senses and instincts to the extent that we begin to question what and who we are. *Early man never had this luxury!* Daily survival by violence precludes explanations for it.

If you can begin to accept yourself as a person deserving your God-given right to exist, free of threats, intimidation, and other people's violence, and if you can concern yourself more with removing your enemy swiftly, brutally, and deadly if need be, without concern with what kind of legal trouble you might get into, you can then begin to become what you already are—*a predator!*

Of the five "families" of kung fu san soo training, the Fut Ga family is entirely offense-oriented in its application. You will be called upon to act swiftly and decisively without hesitation or fear. There is a tendency among a lot of people to hold on tightly to their fears *only because they THINK they lack courage.* Since this seems to be a pervasive attitude among those who are preyed upon with some regularity, let's take a close look at "fear" and "courage" and discover something about yourself to start you on your way.

First of all, fear and courage are relative to the situation and the person. *Fear and courage are the same animal in different clothes!* Find a person who has *had to act* in a moment of greatest fear and you'll discover a hero. Find a person who hasn't had to act in a moment of greatest fear and you will find what society calls a coward. Of course, in my own opinion, the conditions of hero/coward are so subjective and relative to a particular circumstance that the terminology shouldn't even exist.

Depending upon circumstances uniquely our own, we are all both coward and hero. Does this sound confusing? I'll be more specific. I was struck by a particular irony a few years ago, when some friends and I were involved in a discussion about our hobbies and interests. Most of their hobbies ran the gamut from snow and water skiing, sailing, and scuba diving to the usual interests of hunting and fishing.

When I mentioned that my interests involved sky sports, including skydiving, hang gliding, and bungee diving from tall bridges, one of the guys said, "That sure

COURAGE: THE HEART OF A FIGHTER

sounds exciting, but I just don't have the guts to do that kinda stuff myself." I was astonished to hear *him* say this, because his idea of a real swell time was to ride Brahma bulls at rodeos! (There isn't enough money in the world to get me on the back of one of those leaping, man-crushing beasts!)

When viewed objectively, some of these hobbies are considered frightening by most sane people. Yet the *excitement* factor supersedes the fear factor sufficiently enough to allow both him and me to pursue our respective hobbies with relatively little fear. In other words, it doesn't take a great deal of courage for me to dive out of an airplane or my friend to strap himself atop a mad bull, because neither of us are frightened enough not to do it (because of our familiarity). This being the case, neither he or I are to be considered brave or courageous (stupid goes without saying) because we enjoy what we do without too much stress or fear to distract us.

A person displays courage when compelled to act despite fear. It would take a great deal of courage for me to ride the bull, because it frightens more than excites me. Since courage is directly proportionate to the level of fear involved, then it would follow that the more frightened we are, the *greater potential for courage we can muster!*

Of course, I've been talking about dealing with fears of convenience. But confronting fears of convenience goes a long way toward being able to effectively handle fears of necessity. A mastery of a fear of convenience might be to learn how to swim when you're afraid of deep water, learn to fly when you're afraid of heights, or learn to fight when you're afraid of fighting. In each of these instances, you'll be able to vanquish your fears by gaining knowledge about what to do *in actuality* rather than *in the event of* a particular instance.

Think about that for a moment. By taking action to learn what to do in an element that brings you fear, you're equipping yourself with tools to defend against something *that will no longer exist!*

Do you doubt this? Well then, conduct a little experiment to prove me either right or wrong. Think of something that you're afraid of. C'mon, think of something reeeeeally scary. Got it? Now measure it. But wait a minute. How will you measure it? Will you use a ruler? A scale? A bucket? Can you pour fear into a hat? Can you grab it and stuff it in your pocket?

How can you measure something that doesn't exist in the first place?! Fear is an idea, *an emotion,* and not much different in material substance than a wish. A friend of mine from Texas had an appropriate aphorism to put this issue in perspective, in that when I'd said I wished he would disappear, he replied, "Well ah'll tell ya whut, Graig . . . wish in one hand and shit in the other and see which hand fills up quickest." I think fear would take up even less space than a wish in this analogy.

Dealing with fear in a situation of necessity presents a different problem. When we're suddenly confronted with a frightening or shocking situation—e.g., imminent car wreck, house fire, mugging, etc.—we deal with it in an immediate way *because we have to!* And in that moment of spontaneous response, you'll either faint, become immobilized, panic . . . or maintain your composure to do what needs to be done, and in the *doing,* you'll find that place inside you that others call heroic!

What you need to do is find this place within yourself and nurture it, cultivate it, and reap the rewards of your efforts when you've truly made this place in your heart your own. This is accomplished by addressing and conquering progressively larger fears. And while at this moment what I say might sound like just so much rhetoric, I promise you this wellspring of strength and courage exists!

You can begin to fan the flames of your hero's glow this very day, within this very hour if you wish. How? By beginning to rid yourself of the many little fears that have imprisoned you and made you small. Do something right away to bolster your courage and self-esteem by confronting someone whom you allow to minimize you in some small way.

Do this now before you continue with this book. Go to the store, restaurant, bank, or service station and insist on some specific service (only if you normally feel shy or apologetic about it). Don't be bullied or embarrassed; stick to your guns and go over their heads to their boss if need be, but do it! The worst thing that could possibly happen is that you won't get what you already don't have . . . you can't lose!

This is simply a mild foray into the realm of assertion training. Simple though this may be, it's very effective in setting a precedent to begin operating from a position of strength. With inner strength comes self-confidence. With self-confidence comes

courage. When you have this courage, you
begin to realize that you could have done
this a long time ago, and because you could
have done this a long time ago, you should
realize you've always had it, and you have
the potential to have so much more now!

Strength builds on strength, and courage
builds on courage. Each will require some
effort from you, but no more effort than you
can accomplish in a very short time. Fear, on
the other hand, is a strange animal indeed. It
feeds upon itself and encourages its survival
by supplanting the seeds of doubt. Self-
doubt finds fertile soil in a faint heart.

You don't have to be faint of heart! You can
literally change your entire life in the span of a
single second, merely by deciding to do it *and
then ACTING ON IT!* Do you want to be brave?
Do you want to stand up to someone? Do you
really want to *be* the person you wish you
could be? I swear to you that it *is* possible
if–you–will–only DO IT!

DO IT! Two simple words that can
change your life. DO IT isn't simply words;
DO IT is an attitude that can ignite in your
heart with the idea, kindle into flame by the
spoken word or serious intent, and burst
into inferno by *action!*

This is so simple, I know even as I write
this that you'll toy with the concept and
then dismiss it out of hand. But before you
do this, play with the possibilities for awhile
before continuing with this book.

The next time you're affronted by
someone who wants to use you as an
"emotional tampon," and you feel like
telling them to share their woes with
someone who gives a damn, DO IT!

The next time you're getting slow service

at a restaurant, gas station, bank, store, etc.,
because of some person's indifference, and
you want to get on his or her ass about it or
complain to the management, DO IT!

The next time you're in a movie theater
and someone begins to disrupt your
concentration by gabbing with their partner
in the seat behind you, and you want to tell
them to "shuddup," DO IT!

The next time someone gets in your face
for whatever reason and begins yelling and
threatening you, and you want to punch
him in the nose, don't even think about it—
DO IT!

If you're feeling trapped by staying in a
dead-end job, town, marriage, etc., consider
what you'd really rather be doing to make
your life happy, and for God's sake, DO IT!

What about the repercussions of your
actions, you say? What if you're arrested for
punching someone in the nose, taken to the
cleaners in a divorce, bankrupt for quitting
the dead-end job, evicted from the theater
for yelling shuddup, or asked to leave the
store for demanding more than they're
willing to give?

These are all good questions you might
ask, and the answer to them is simple—SO
WHAT?! Remember, in the worst case, you
won't get what you already don't have, so
you can't lose there, and in a best case,
you'll get what you want!

While it may be true that you didn't
want to be arrested, bankrupt, asked to
leave, or lose a friend, you will have gained
inner strength, and courage to act, sufficiently enough to reward your courage in
action to DO IT. Because regardless of the
consequences, you will have taken

command of your own life to attain the destiny of your choice.

And while there might be inherent obstacles like those mentioned above, at least you will have created a change in conditions so that the person who was in your face getting rowdy won't take such liberties with you again. You'll find a new and better job or spouse, and you'll operate from a position of strength when dealing with people. But much more beyond this, *you will have gained respect for yourself!* You'll make active decisions in your life to do what you want and get what you want.

Another kind of fear to be dealt with in a potentially combative situation is the fear of decisive action. Though this sounds simple in print, it becomes much more complex when you examine it more closely. Let's look closer and find out why this kind of fear is actually the key to unlocking the rest of the self-imposed shackles that inhibit someone.

In order to take a decisive action, you're really doing several things simultaneously. First, you recognize that you *must* take action, and with this thought comes a fear of commitment. You consider that if you commit yourself to this action (initiating an attack), you leave yourself exposed to a physical reprisal. This is understandable but also dangerous— dangerous because of the likelihood that your opponent is going to attack you anyway, whether you initiate an attack or not, and in your indecision, you will be struck.

If you decide to act on a little courage and sort of lash out at your opponent and kinda hope you beat him and utter a silent prayer that everything will work out fine, then I can safely promise you that it won't. Your body

English, in word, action, and deed, will betray you, and you will end up bleeding.

Take confidence in your physical abilities to get the job done, and then DO IT! There won't be any reprisal because your enemy/opponent/fear will be vanquished and therefore pose no more threat to you. This will happen because your mind (courage and conviction) is your superior weapon. Your force of will to attack, which will be both sudden and violent in the extreme, will save your life. All of this is on a primal level, *and you have this ability within you right now!*

Another psychological block that prevents some people from making a decisive act and committing to the action is the ramifications of what they do and how this unknown factor will affect their lives.

For instance, if you're confronted by someone who you know is very likely going to attack you, you might try to reason your way out of it in hopes that you might diffuse the situation and therefore not end up in either A) the hospital or B) jail.

Again, this line of reasoning is at the same time understandable and dangerous. Understandable, because you don't want to go to either the hospital or jail, and danger-ous because in the time it takes for this idea to occur to you and for you to consider it, BAAAM! You'll be hit and going to the hospital anyway! The future will take care of itself, good or bad, with or without your consideration. So, in a combative situation, be completely alive, aware, spontaneous and decisive in both mind and action.

Now that you've practiced asserting yourself in places and situations sufficient to allow yourself the courage and dignity not to allow anyone to threaten or intimidate you anymore, you can begin to hone the sting and stun of your weapons and unleash the breath of the dragon—your intrinsic rage!

Bottled up inside everyone is a hurricane of suppressed hostility and violence. Because we live in what is ostensibly a civilized society, these feelings are never given vent because we *just know that we'll black out and kill someone!*

If you really believe this, then you don't ever have to worry about anyone else victimizing you *because you're doing a better job of it yourself!* Think about it for a moment. Hiding behind this "blackout" excuse lurks a sinister parasite to your power that you dress in sheep's clothing and call a conscience.

Keep in mind as you read this that the situation of an all-out violent encounter with someone—where it's okay to drop that thin veneer of civility long enough to open that Pandora's box in which you hide your primal rage and passions—*is being brought to you anyway, whether–you–like–it–or–not!* Conscience has no role to play in an encounter such as this. You must do this to survive!

Most sane people are aware of the difference between good and bad and can exercise a modicum of judgment to make an intelligent decision about what to do in a given instance. I'm making a presumption that you, the reader, have this ability, and can distinguish between a situation where

THE RAGE OF AN INNER BEAST

you're merely being taunted and one where your life is being threatened.

If you're in a situation where you can leave at any time, regardless of the state of your pride or ego, you can embrace the values accorded by your conscience and be proud of the fact that you did. Take pride and comfort as a person of great merit that you don't have to "prove" anything to yourself or to another.

The instances I'll be referring to throughout the rest of this text will concern situations where you *must act quickly* to save your life or someone else's. In situations such as these (and I invite you to conjure up your own scenarios where this would be the case), you will find it of tremendous advantage to develop a *concentrated and focused rage.*

We've been taught for years to keep a cool head under stress, and that "flying into a rage" is to be avoided at all costs, because it impairs thinking. The problem with this rationale is that in an encounter where you're essentially fighting for your life, *you don't have time to think.* In the midst of extreme violence, there is only action. Remember, we aren't talking about a sport here, where you can have the luxury of a referee, strategy from the corner, and rules to protect you.

The true champions of any sport are those who have emerged victorious time after time while in the heat of battle, whatever battle that might be. They've found and focused their rage to win spontaneously *in the doing of the battle!* A lot of athletes have the skill, knowledge, strength, speed, and experience to win, but in the final analysis, it will be the heart of the warrior, the rage, that will determine the final outcome.

Rage can be viewed in the same way as an explosion. Rage or explosives in and of themselves can be harmless or destructive beyond belief. Let's examine this corollary a little closer.

If you throw a large firecracker into the air to explode, it will cause little more damage than a lot of noise, *in much the same way as striking your thumb with a hammer* (and the noise you make).

If you set a large firecracker onto the ground to explode, it will do little more than make noise and leave a hole in the ground, *in much the same way as then smashing the hammer onto the table* (to get even with the hammer).

If you place a large firecracker under a bowl, the energy will be more focused, and the explosion will make noise and send the bowl high into the air, *in much the same way as hurling the hammer through the window* (causing the missus to jump high into the air).

Ultimately, you can think of a concentrated and focused rage, coupled with knowledge of fighting skills, as being similar to a demolition job. Placing explosive charges at strategic locations on a large building can drop it onto and within itself without endangering the surroundings. Though the explosion is violent in the extreme, the *concentration* and the *focus* of the explosion/raging forces is still *controlled,* even though it might appear otherwise. This is enough to make a formerly Herculean task look simple in its aftermath.

It's important to fully understand at this point that when I refer to an explosive rage to propel your attack into an opponent, I'm not talking about getting *angry* at your attacker and therefore directing your *anger* at him, thus being controlled by that very anger in return. The inner rage that I refer to is that primal instinct of the predator within.

Consider the wolverine for a moment. The name alone is synonymous with ferocity. The wolverine is a member of the weasel family, stands a foot high at the shoulders, and weighs between 30 and 50 pounds. Despite the small size of the wolverine, *its ferocity is such that it is well known to take food from mountain lions and bears!* This single-mindedness of purpose and ferocious behavior is something we all are capable of.

The wolverine, and every other predatory animal, utilizes this sudden and terrible rage as a necessity to survival. Animals don't regard their inner rage as being a weapon or a tool any more than we would consider the neuromuscular activity necessary to pick up a glass of water. We–just–DO IT!

What gets in the way of our own single-mindedness of purpose is our very own thought processes. We're always considering the consequences of a plethora of possibilities, e.g., "Is he going to hit me? If I hit him first and he gets hurt, will I have to go to jail? Can I talk my way out of this? Should I just run? Maybe I should just go ahead and hit him and get it over with. But what if I lose? What if I get get hurt and have to go to the hospital? I can't afford to miss any work, and besides, what will I say when my friends see me with my face all messed up? To hell with it, he can't bully me like that, who does he think he's messin' with anyway? I'm just gonna kick his BAM BAM BAAAMM! (Silence and darkness. *You've just been knocked out!*)

The longer you stay in a contemplative mode, considering implied and actual risk, the more vulnerable you become because of your indecision to act. Specifically, if a potentially violent situation is brought to you, and you *think* that you might have to hit an aggressor to abort his attack, DO IT!

Because of the offensive mode of predatory training, you must now change in your mind and in your heart your attitude toward an opponent. From now on, the only acceptable words for your opponent will be either "victim" or "prey." No other words will suffice.

The reason for this is both psychological and practical. It is psychological because it will remove from you the anxiety of a "fight." The anxiety won't be present because there will be no fight—your "victim" won't have that opportunity! The practical side of this issue is merely semantic. The word "opponent" implies a state of mutual combat. Mutual combat cannot occur in a condition of predator/prey. It is merely a doomed struggle for survival for your prey.

W hen you're confronted by someone who insists on becoming a victim, before you can oblige him, you must learn to apply certain basic principles of line, distance, angle, and movement of attack. These principles and applications are covered more extensively in my first book, *Sudden Violence: The Art of San Soo*, published by Paladin Press.

The principles of line, distance, angle, and movement of attack are the essence of common denominators to be found in any situation where physical violence can occur. Application of these principles is effective because the physics behind them are sound.

In this chapter, I'll provide you with a rudimentary understanding of the principles of fighting and show you how to use them. I encourage you to re-read this chapter when you come to the end of it, and begin to apply what you've learned with a partner.

To begin, it's paramount that you have a thorough understanding of the distance principle. There is a natural safe distance between you and your victim that will accord you some latitude for choice in how you'll attack him. The distance I'm speaking of is the length of your outstretched arm to your victim's chest. This distance is critical, because, should your prey elect to strike you first, anything less than arm's length will leave you vulnerable to a sucker punch due to the loss of reaction time.

When you allow your prey to get closer than arm's length, you'll also be giving him the opportunity to employ whatever speed or closing skills he might have, such as sucker punching, headbutting, or tackling. *This is unacceptable!* You are a predator;

don't ever forget that. A–predator–does–not–allow–himself–to–become–prey! As a predator, you cannot allow your prey the luxury of even the smallest advantage.

Equally important is not allowing your prey to get beyond your arm's reach. If you allow him to do so, he will have several advantages. He can feint, maneuver for position, punch or kick with maximum force, produce a weapon, or launch a complex attack (punches and kicks followed by a sweep or tackle).

As a predator, you will attack your prey at the very first movement. If a situation arises that you feel is dangerous, then it should be of little importance whether that movement was to pick his nose or throw a punch. Remember, a stranger becomes prey, and subsequently a victim, when he brings the threat of violence to you. If you did nothing to provoke a stranger into becoming your prey, your conscience can remain clear.

Once your safe distance of arm's reach is determined and established, strive to maintain it. If your prey begins to get "froggy" by puffing up his chest and bobbing up and down, and he begins to backpedal a little bit to allow himself some room to maneuver, follow him. Become his shadow and don't allow him out of your reach. If he begins to crowd you by invading your safe distance, attack him. He has unwittingly provided you with the timing and opportunity to neutralize and abort his aggression because he will have reduced his own reaction time to your attack.

Generally, if you have the latitude to attack at your own discretion (90 percent of the time you will), you'll find it to your advantage to have a reliable and natural thought/action scenario to enact when you determine the time is right.

One of the vague notions that students of practically any endeavor are advised to follow is, "Do whatever feels right to you." But then you might ask, "When do I do it?" Of course, the predictable response would be, "Whenever it feels right to you." It's because of this vagueness that I'll describe a simple, direct, and effective means of whetting your predatory appetite to be able to carry through whatever you plan to do.

Since you won't want effective resistance from your prey, it would be in your interest to make your entry into or into and alongside him. These are your lines of attack. If you step deep enough into him so that you end up pelvis to pelvis with enough force to knock him off balance, you will have taken his balance and inhibited his mobility. At the same time as you make your entry, you will pin his arms to his sides, leaving you in opportune position to headbutt, bite, run in place up into his groin, and all kinds of other fun stuff, as you'll come to learn. By stepping into the middle of him and doing these things, you will have effectively aborted his attack and immobilized his fighting tools. You can also step deeply into and alongside your prey to end up behind him, thereby avoiding his fighting tools. Once you're there, there's a wide variety of options open to you that I'll go into in further detail later on as well.

If you choose to go alongside and behind him, you will need to do so with the most efficient body mechanics possible. To do that, you must first consider a few things about his body in relation to yours immediately before you attack.

If you stand in front of someone and look at his feet, you'll notice that invariably there will be one foot slightly forward of the other (your own included). To use this to your advantage, notice which of his feet is nearest you and then "mirror" that foot with your own. For instance, if his right foot is forward, you should shift your position (without being obvious) so that your left foot is in a direct line with his right foot.

The reason for this is simple; it gives you a ready choice of where to make your entry and shortens the distance you'll travel to get behind him. Additionally, whichever side of your prey you decide to enter, step to that side with the corresponding leg. For instance, if you're going to step to the left of him, step in with your left leg. If you're going to step to the right of him, step in with your right leg.

Once you've established your safe distance (arm's length) and mirrored his posture, you can then "image" your prey. "Imaging" involves looking intently at his body picture/image and fixing it in your mind so that any deviation from this image will trigger your attack. This serves a few purposes. It will concentrate your attention to the exclusion of all else, so that no outside distraction such as self-doubt, confusion, or anything else will deter you from your prey's image. A break, any little break, in his image should trigger your attack.

During your training with your partner, develop a "hungry eye" to focus more intently than you are ever normally called upon to do. Watch for such things as a dip of his head, a deep breath—*any movement whatsoever should prompt you to attack him!*

So, here you are minding your own business, thinking how cool it'll be when you finally win the big lottery, or get that big inheritance, or when any number of celebrities finally come to their collective senses and come to you demanding that you make love to them until you melt like butter, when all of a sudden there stands before you a massive brute whose shouting snaps you out of your reverie. (It seems you've decided to lean against his new car while you indulged in these various fantasies.) Naturally you apologize, but this isn't good enough for your new-found friend. He makes it clear, through verbal and physical threats, that he's going to "teach you a lesson you'll never forget."

What will you do? If fleeing isn't an option, and it becomes apparent that he's going to attack you, you don't have time to weigh your decisions and consequences. You'll be hit long before then.

As subtly as you can, by shifting your position while making the placating gestures he's expecting, establish your safe distance, choose an avenue of entry, image him even if he's wildly throwing his arms around, and attack him in the very instant he moves from the photo image in your brain at whatever position his arms or legs were in.

As a predator, you don't have the time or inclination to philosophize. You can't have any concern for how much you injure your prey. You can't afford the self-indulgent luxury of remorse, for if you indulge in it at all, you'll effectively lose your hungry eye as a predator. In the moment you lose your edge as a predator, you will become prey.

The danger in immersing yourself in your

predator abilities and then turning your back on them is that you will become vulnerable to your ego. Ego in this light is disastrous because it will give you a false sense of security. For instance, if you recently gave vent to your predatory nature by decimating someone who ordinarily would have frightened you, it will be very easy for your mind/ego to say, "Boy I really kicked his ass. I'm one bad mutha!"

Being a predator is a state of being, *not a state of mind.* If you begin to feel that you're really tough and can afford the heroic moments of making a fool out of someone you're about to engage in combat with, you–will–be–a–victim! Why? Maybe your opponent is in a larger predatory mode than you. While you're boasting, he'll be watching you . . . hungrily!

HONE THE FANGS, SHARPEN THE CLAWS

"Is a predator always a predator?"

"If I learn predation skills, will they always be there for me?"

"I mean, like if I learn to do all this predator stuff, will I be dangerous to be around? (I hope I hope!)"

"I don't have to go and kill a cow and sleep inside its stomach or anything, do I?"

"What the hell is a predator anyway?"

If by definition you feel comfortable with the title "couch potato" and feel little inclination to change your sedentary lifestyle, then give this book to someone else. It won't do you any good until you're ready to do yourself some good by getting up off your ass to take charge of your life! DO IT! Do it *now*. Begin by getting up and reading this while you're standing and pacing.

Life is a verb! Life is *action* that is realized through you and through your active participation in it. You help to liberate the predator within you by being more alert and more attuned to your immediate environment. Being a predator is a full-time job!

Think of the last time you were radiantly alive. Could it have been a near-miss auto collision? Perhaps an airplane ride that you just knew you wouldn't survive? Maybe it was a combat experience, or a fistfight you almost had, or a roller coaster ride, or anything else that frightened, shook, or exhilarated you.

Close your eyes and capture again that "moment." If you can do that, then take the time to stay in that moment and realize how much more *focused* you were then than at any other time in your life.

When you are completely focused in the moment, life becomes a little larger than what it was only seconds ago. Think about it—weren't colors a little bit brighter? Didn't the flowers smell a little more fragrant? Didn't the actual event seem to happen in slow motion? And when you were able to get your heartbeat and respiration back to normal, you didn't notice these things at all anymore but rather dwelled on the "awful" event until all else was blocked out.

As a predator, you will be called upon to live more in the moment than you ever thought possible. Ironically, once you realize your personal potential as a predator and can live fully in the moment, where nothing escapes your attention, *you won't want to live any other way.*

There's a great difference between a predator in the zoo and a predator in the wild. The predator in the zoo doesn't have to stalk and kill its prey. The predator in the zoo is fed on a regular basis, gets very little of the exercise it would get in the wild, and in essence has become fat and lazy.

As a society, we've become fat and lazy. That doesn't mean that either we or the zoo predator isn't dangerous; it simply means that we aren't as efficient as we can be. It also means that as lazy as we've gotten, if we had to rely on our predator instincts in the wild, be it in the jungle or the street, *we could die!* In order to rectify this dangerous situation, you'll need to regain the predator's heart and allow the beast within to emerge.

To do this, you'll need sufficient reflexes to carry your weapons to your prey without being detected. One of the surest ways to develop a foundation to build upon will be to take up an activity that will enhance fast-twitch muscle response. What I mean by a fast-twitch muscle response is a sudden,

explosive burst of action as is required in
sports such as racquetball, tennis, football,
basketball, etc. One principal difference
between what you'll be doing and what
occurs in the sports I've mentioned is that
they utilize the fast-twitch muscle response
in a sudden change of direction while
they're already in motion. You, on the other
hand, will employ the fast-twitch response
to *initiate motion*.

To hone your awareness skills and, by
extension, your awareness as a predator, I'm
going to prescribe for you an exercise to
perform with a partner. You will do this
exercise in five-minute intervals and then
trade positions with your partner. I don't
want you to continue past five minutes on
one facet of the exercise, because five
minutes will be an initial peak for you to
reach while keeping your concentration up.
Beyond five minutes, the mind will tend to
wander. The very instant your mind begins
to wander, *stop* and continue *only* when
you're focused and alert.

Get a ball of some kind. Start with one the
size of a soccer or basketball and then ad-
vance down to the size of a baseball. Have
your partner stand on a chair holding the ball
while you stand arm's reach away from him/
her. Make a mark with bright tape or colored
marker on an object immediately across from
your partner to indicate a level from the top
of the head to the top of the chest of your
imaginary prey. Once this is done, simply
have your partner drop the ball from the
height of the head mark. You should stand in
a normal, relaxed posture, then suddenly
explode in to catch the ball before it gets
below the lowest point you have marked.

To get the most from this exercise, don't fix your gaze on the ball itself, but rather look in the area between the marks. You can have one foot slightly forward of the other, with feet shoulder width apart. Once the ball is dropped, thrust forward by launching off with the ball of your trailing foot. Concentrate on not making any overt movements in shifting of your weight, balance, or facial expression when you lunge in to catch it.

The principal goal in this exercise is to be able to explode into and/or alongside your prey with minimal telegraphic movement. During the course of this particular exercise, you should feel where your best position of explosive entry is in relation to your position of balance. Find this place through as many repetitions as it takes so that you won't have to A) shift balance, B) step in, and C) attack. Do the exercise to the point where all you need do is *attack!*

I encourage you to make variations of this exercise, create for yourself similar exercises that will enhance the qualities of fast-twitch response, and encourage subtle yet explosive entries. In the performing process of an exercise, develop and learn to trust a "hungry eye" toward any peripheral movement. Better that you should jump the gun a little bit when you execute a movement than get caught by surprise and let an object get past you.

In addition to practicing movement skills to enter and occupy your prey, you will need the necessary grip strength to keep him in your talons. To this end, you will need to work on your gripping strength by whatever means possible. Possibilities include continually squeezing a ball of rubber, clay, or wax, or use a spring or heavy-gauge gripper designed especially for grip strength. But whatever you get, *use it!* Use it often and use it for long periods of time. At the completion of a strengthening session, be sure to stretch and work on the flexibility of your wrists and fingers; this is equally important.

If you were a race car driver, you would want your car in top running condition before a race. As a predator, you will have to be ready to allow the beast within to emerge at any moment. If the inner beast is given free reign when you need it most, wouldn't it be a good idea to make available the necessary weapons when it needs them (strength, speed, flexibility)?

If you had a panther at your side ready and willing to do your bidding when your safety was in peril, you would take the time to feed and nurture the animal so that it would protect you. It would follow then that as a predator you will make the necessary effort to eat nutritious foods and maintain physical fitness to bring into *being* that which already exists in your heart, and walk with the pride and dignity that is rightfully yours!

It's a beautiful starlit night, replete with the fragrance of springtime blossoms and the sounds of birds flitting from treetop to rooftop. Against the gentle background of soft puffy clouds and brilliant stars twinkling there's a feeling in the air of peace and contentment. It's the kind of night that makes you smile with sweet memories and sigh in wonder with the wistful yearnings of the future. Wouldn't it be nice if you . . . WHAM BAM BAAAM!

Hi. I can see you're awake now. Are you feeling better? Man that was some beating you took. You look like hell on a stick. I was going to say something to you about that guy lounging in the doorway of that shop, but I figured you were paying attention. I figured, what the heck, you being a predator and all, you'd be much more aware and would intercept and remove him. There was even a terrific brick wall behind him and everything. What's that you say? What good would the wall have done you? I'm glad you asked that question, because that's going to be the topic of this chapter.

I'll mention first that you can't afford the luxury of becoming so absorbed in the *ambience* of your environment that you exclude the detail of your surroundings. As a predator, you must be ever aware of the pulse and tick around you at all times.

As for the ability to use the wall behind your prey, it will be necessary to pay special attention to the entry skills and line of attack principles you learned in *Sudden Violence*, particularly to plunging into and alongside your prey in order to maneuver and propel him into the wall (or other object).

Begin now by having your partner stand with the wall at his back while you stand in front of him (fig. 1). Since your prey still

MANEUVERING YOUR PREY

Figure 1

Figure 2

Figure 3

thinks he's the predator, he will be watching you intently so that if you move to either side of him, he will reposition himself so that you will remain in what he thinks is the better position to attack you. This being the case, stand directly in front of him *only* if the wall is directly behind him. If not, position yourself in front of him in such a way that he will have the wall to his back.

Notice which of your partner's feet is slightly forward of the other, and shift your nearest foot closest to it. For instance, if he's standing with his right foot slightly forward, then have your left foot slightly forward so that you will have a clean avenue of entry, as seen in Figure 1. Now, launch into and alongside his right side with your left leg deeply enough that you can look behind his head (fig. 2).

At his point, you'll have your left foot behind and between his legs, with your right hand going to the hair at the top of his head and your left hand clutching his shirt or jacket at the back of his neck. You will then bring your right leg around so that you are now on the opposite side of him (fig. 3). You yank back and down with his hair as you pull him to slam the top of his skull into the wall (easy on your partner) (figs. 4, 5).

This is a good basic technique in which

Figure 4   *Figure 5*

to practice an entry that will allow you to rotate around your opponent while utilizing the wall to inflict the majority of damage or at least enough body shock to your prey to allow you time to concentrate your attack.

I must remind you again that these predatory principles and techniques are designed to bring a great deal of pain and injury to your prey. And since physical trauma will be your stock in trade, *you must be absolutely certain within your own conscience that physical force is imminent, so that you must initiate violence to protect yourself!*

When you determine that a situation requires you to let loose the beast, you *must* be decisive! You *must* act fast! And, you *must be ruthless!* There is no state of being as "kind of a predator." Make your decision with the commitment to see it through, and don't even think of releasing your prey if there's a single wiggle left in him.

Another way to utilize the wall behind your prey would be to make essentially the same entry as the first technique (into and alongside of him, to your left), but as you pull yourself into him with your left hand, cup his chin with your right hand as you make your deep entry (fig. 6).

In one fluid movement, step your right leg wide around and behind, pivot on your left foot (fig. 7), and power drive his face into the wall (fig. 8).

Another option would be to step deep between his legs with your right leg as you headbutt his face. As you headbutt, grab/slide your hands down along his arms to abort his counter and to grab the back sides of his pants (fig. 9).

Your headbutt will start his momentum

Figure 6

Figure 8

Figure 7

Figure 9

backward toward the wall so that when
you give a big yank on his pants, the back
of his head will snap backward, striking the
wall (fig. 10).

Yet another possibility would be to step
to the left and alongside him with your left
foot as you pull his right arm to you with

Figure 10   *Figure 11*

your left hand. Capture his pulled arm with
your right hand too as you pull him to you
(fig. 11), then pivot around behind him to
drop onto your right knee, pulling on his
arm to propel his face into the wall (figs. 12,
13, 14).

For simplicity of example, I use the brick
wall as a guideline for facilitating the above
techniques. These can and should be
modified as the need dictates and should be
readily adaptable to using on automobiles,
plate glass windows, light poles, or similar
objects as backdrops sufficient to effect a
traumatic injury. As you can see when you
practice these techniques, the net result of
using a solid backdrop can be particularly
grisly when you crush your prey's head and
face into it with the force necessary to
neutralize him.

The important thing for you to focus on
as you practice this training and these
techniques is your attitude in *the doing of it*.
Being a predator is more a matter of being

Figure 12

Figure 13

Figure 14

one at heart and remembering a natural
state than studiously attempting to emulate
something you don't really think you can
be. Being a predator is much more than
being an animal willing to tear someone to
shreds given the situation and the oppor-

tunity. *Being a predator is truly a way of life!*

People who consider themselves as prey regard life as a noun, a condition consisting of people, places, and things. A predator *knows* life is a verb! Life–is–action! Where prey sees a threat, *a predator sees dinner.* Prey will say, "I hope he doesn't hurt me." Predators will say, "One foot closer and I'll have your ass!"

There are so many who believe their condition of prey to be permanent. WRONG! You are a product of your beliefs, perspectives, and perceptions. Do you believe me? If you don't, then humor me by taking stock of who and what you believe you are, and answer these few simple questions.

    A) Are you male or female?
    B) Are you white, black, Hispanic?
    C) What's your occupation?
    D) What's your religion?
    E) Are you predator or prey?

For the sake of illustration, let's suppose someone answering this query answers MALE-WHITE-CLERK-PROTES-TANT-PREY. In essence, our case model considers himself to be a white male protestant clerk who believes himself to be prey. Do you think so too? Is he nothing else? Remember, who a person is isn't necessarily what a person is. Our case model views himself differently than a Jivaro indian (headhunter), lion, or medical student would see him. For instance, they would believe our case model to be the following:

	MALE	WHITE	CLERK	PROTESTANT	PREY
Headhunter					
	shrunken head	white shrunken head	shrunken head	shrunken head	shrunken head
Lion					
	meat	light meat	meat	meat	meat
Medical Student					
	cadaver	cadaver	cadaver	cadaver	cadaver

We begin making distinctions by and of ourselves. If you believe being a male makes a big difference in everything, it will (may not necessarily be true).

If you believe being white makes a big difference in all that matters, it will (even though to the rest of the world it may not).

If you believe being wealthy is the only important thing in life, it will be. (I'd like to be wealthy too!)

If you believe being a Baptist is paramount to one's salvation, it will be (but not to the headhunter, lion, or student).

If you believe you are prey, you will be. But you *can* change your mind about that. Think not? Then consider this.

Have you ever snuck up on a fly and swatted it? Have you ever crept up to a stream to catch a fish? Have you ever simply crept up to a butterfly to catch it? Being a predator is inherent with the human condition. If you want to *be* a predator, simply live and think as one. You aren't really learning to be a predator, *I'm simply reminding you!*

W hen does the predator become prey? When is a predator most vulnerable? Does a predator know when to back down? Can a predator ever be too confident? How many opponents are too many?

These are questions you might be asking right about now, and it's a good way get started into the next phase of your training. So when does a predator become prey? A predator becomes prey *when a predator allows himself to become prey.* If you stay alert, assertive, and aware, you're in a predator's natural state. If you become lazy in your thoughts, awareness, and body, you'll regress to being prey.

When is a predator most vulnerable? A predator is vulnerable when he isn't focused *entirely in the moment.* At that point, by not paying attention, in the span of seconds *he becomes prey.* A predator never accords anyone that opportunity!

Does a predator know when to back down? Yes. But more specifically, a predator will be aware of the pulse and tempo of those around him, to either avoid trouble *without having to back down* or, when trouble is unavoidable, introduce a whole new definition of trouble to his prey.

Can a predator ever be too confident? No. If one is truly a predator (not just "kind of a predator"), confidence is a fuel that allows him or her to take decisive action without hesitation.

How many opponents are too many? I think a better question would be, "When are too many opponents *not enough?*" Only time, place, circumstance, and the ferocity to engage can determine when a predator overextends his abilities.

WHEN PREY IS PLENTIFUL

Figure 15

Figure 16

To more fully explore the potential and possibilities in harvesting more than one prey, you must be completely comfortable in your knowledge and application of the principles of line, distance, angle, and movement of attack. When you do this, it might surprise you to find that rather than dealing with several individuals, you'll be handling an extension of a single victim that will draw in the others in a smooth flow of movement.

To better illustrate the value of leading, drawing, and weaving one victim into another, let's explore some possibilities in a technique involving two victims-to-be.

In this scenario, there are two menacing teenagers. (I use teenagers in this example because it's a situation that demands discretion and a firm hand to avoid taking a life—an action you might not be so reluctant to take if they were adults and armed, as the teens are.)

In this example (fig. 15), you would "mirror" the stance of the prey nearest you. By doing this, you're picking an avenue of entry that's going to place you in a strategic position to deal with your next victim when you make your initial move. You might then take control of his arm and buckle his leg to abort his mobility, gain an entry, and place him between you and your next victim (fig. 16).

You would then effect a lock on your prey's hair as you occupied his center of gravity (this should be a single, fluid movement as you practice it). This allows you to control and direct one of your victims into the other if need be (fig. 17).

Once you press your initial victim into the other, you're in position to reach over

Figure 17

Figure 18

and effect a hair lock/control technique to direct the center of gravity of your next victim's body over your first victim's (fig. 18) to put you in better position to hurt him.

By utilizing a hair control technique to keep them both in place, you can shift your trailing leg around and behind to tighten your control of them by compacting their centers of gravity. This will serve to put you in a progressively better position (fig. 19).

By torquing your torso on around in the same movement and direction, you can topple them over your leg to take them down (fig. 20).

You can continue by dropping to your knee to better facilitate your takedown, and shifting your hands to acquire a better grip of their hair to maintain your control (fig. 21).

You can then use their hair as a come-

Figure 19

Figure 20

Figure 21

along, or you can kick to their thighs and biceps to immobilize them and deter their pursuit should you elect not to hurt them too badly (fig. 22).

This technique is merely an exercise in application of known principles of attack. There will be a wide margin for spontaneity when you practice this and other techniques at speed.

Of greatest importance to you in a "prey harvest" will be your attention to small but important detail before you commit yourself to a course of action. One of the important details you will want to focus on will be your initial direction in your attack. For instance, if you had prey on either side of you (fig. 23), the ideal movement would be to the outside of one of them so that you would have the first one that you capture

Figure 22

Figure 23

Figure 24

Figure 25

placed between you and your next victim
(fig. 24). This would accord you the
opportunity of having possession of one of
them at the outset without having to fight
both of them at once (fig. 25).

Even though it might not be to your optimum advantage, you can still fight effectively from between them if you stalk to
within easy range of your nearest prey, gain
a quick entry, and move in to pivot his body
around yours to place him between you and
your next victim (figs. 26, 27, 28). From this
position, you'll be able to injure the prey
you have hold of, or use him as a momentary shield while you maneuver him in
position to acquire your next one (fig. 29).

You have a unique advantage when you
elect to harvest multiple prey. Your victims-
to-be believe themselves to be the aggres-
sors. As such, they will have the mistaken

Figure 26

Figure 27

Figure 28

Figure 29

belief that you will fear them because of their number. Therefore, they won't really regard you as a viable threat. And since they won't believe you to be a threat, they will make some very grave errors in judgment.

Their first mistake will be their decision to screw around with *you!* And what makes *you* so special? You're special because you're motivated to learn how to *be* what you already are. You're finding out through various channels you've explored before you picked up my book—other books, videos, self-defense classes, or other types of training on how to fight. You're also special because of your interest in predator training. As you will have found out by now, being a predator goes against long-taught martial arts dogma about being the aggressor. To them, your being a predator makes you a lesser person, lacking all the wonderful ideals and sportsmanlike, gentlemanly behavior they want to teach you.

What they lose sight of is the fact that you don't take up a *fighting* style so you'll be a pillar in the community. You learn to fight so that you can protect yourself the best way that you can, so that you'll get hurt as little as possible. And so, if you're willing to hurt someone severely, without hesitation, *you won't need a martial art style!*

It's with this thought in mind that I tell you honestly that there's a vast difference between a martial artist and a fighter. If I could choose someone to be at my side in a "prey harvest," I would more readily choose you, whoever you are, sight unseen, than an accomplished and highly ranked martial artist. Why? Because, as I said earlier, you picked up a book that appealed to the predator within and have no delusions about the nobility of your opponent. You're more concerned about your physical well-being than about honor and ethics. I mean this as a compliment, and I congratulate you on your choice. *Predators are survivors!*

Getting back to our prey harvest, let's

Figure 30

Figure 31

look at a few more possibilities. In a situation with two victims-to-be, you would still assess your distance, stalk to optimum range (arm distance), mirror the stance of the prey nearest you, and image him (fig. 30).

Burst into and alongside him to occupy his center of gravity. Control the axial skeleton by securing his upper torso through the trapping of his upper arms and pulling him into you (fig. 31).

Step deep between his legs to be in good position to propel him into your next victim (fig. 32) while maintaining control.

Drive him hard into your other prey at waist level to effect a lean-in torso that will bring him into your circle of influence, which will make a hair control technique accessible (fig. 33).

Establish a good lock on his hair to place

Figure 32

Figure 33

Figure 34

him atop his partner as you step in with
your other leg to tighten control (fig. 34).

Maintaining your hair control on the top
victim, force them both down to a squat as
you step over their bodies (fig. 35).

Drop your weight down hard on them to
let their air out, and then do with them what
you will. Be creative (fig. 36).

Again, these techniques are only food for
thought. That's all a lesson or technique can
ever be, because no two instances will ever
be alike. However, you can gain a sense of
fluidity and momentum if you follow the
mechanics of the techniques as they are
described. Feel free to improvise once your
movement skills are fast and feel natural.

When you're presented with three or four
prey (fig. 37), you can attack in several
directions at once to disperse them enough

Figure 35

Figure 36

Figure 37

Figure 38

to take control of one, to gather in another
to injure and propel into another, and/or to
acquire and injure the other (fig. 38). *Important to remember*—your prey is as motivated
to the harvest as you are, so you *must* act
fast, you *must* hit hard, and you *must* be
deadly accurate when attempting this move!

While you can be completely spontaneous
in your attacks when you harvest your prey,
you will still need to pay strict attention to important details like line, distance, angle, and
movement of attack. These principles are the
common denominators in any fight scenario,
and if you can control and direct your prey into
the parameters that you establish for them, then
you can strike and harvest in complete confidence. You can be the proverbial wolf in
sheep's clothing, while your prey believe
(mistakenly) they're going to have lamb chops.

Tthere he is, standing in front of you describing the many and various ways he's going to kick your ass. Being the predator that you are, and knowing the best opportunity you're ever going to get to kick *his* ass is right now, you punch him as hard as you can, knocking him on his butt several feet from you. But what's this? He's a little stunned, *but not so stunned that he can't grab that beer bottle laying on the sidewalk, break it, and come after you with murder in his eyes!*

You feel a stream of ice water pour into the pit of your stomach as he closes in on you. You're confident enough to know that you can still beat him, *but you also know there's a good chance of getting gashed with his broken bottle before it's all over!*

So now you ask yourself where you went wrong. Didn't you blast him with a killer punch that should have knocked him out? And wasn't that a solid blow? Gee, you did everything that guy that wrote that predator book said you should, and now here's this animal coming at you with a broken bottle. Where did you go wrong?!

This is as good a place to begin seizing your prey as any. And I will say that as long as you hit your prey hard and often, you can't go wrong. However, there are better options available to you than what you elected to do in the above scenario.

What happened in that scenario is what most people will do when they decide to strike first. The only real problem with just knocking the crap out of someone with everything you have is that it knocks him *away from you.* Not only that, but it also serves to give him enough distance from

SEIZE THE PREY

55

you to pick up an object/weapon or to pull a knife or gun from his pocket.

The only real option you might have exercised after knocking him away from you is to follow him and not let him get more than arm's length away. Since you'll be arm's distance from him, you might as well hit him again and again.

An ideal way to strike and seize your prey is to utilize complementary movement. A complementary movement gathers in your prey as you strike. For instance, when you simply punched your prey in the face, it propelled him away from you, thereby dissipating energy from the force of your blow. Had you instead grabbed his upper arm or shirt front to pull him to you as you punched him, you would have increased the power of your blow *and kept him close at hand for further blows without letting him get away.*

To get a better idea of complementary movement and application, I'm going to walk you through a few examples and let you build on them yourself. So, get together with your partner now, and let's explore some possibilities.

Begin by establishing your safe distance from your partner, and visualize your avenues of entry into and alongside his body. For this first example, step in and to the left of him as you pull his upper arm to you to better propel yourself beside him. This is no different than the other entries you've practiced before, but as you do this, give him a right elbow strike to his biceps as you pull him in with your left hand (fig. 39).

Ideally, you'll get several things happening at once. You will want to time your

Figure 39   **Figure 40**

step into him with your grab and strike so
that they seem to happen simultaneously. It's
important when you make an elbow strike to
your prey's muscle that you use the actual
point of the elbow rather than the bottom of
your forearm near your elbow. Feel this
difference and you'll know why immediately.

In keeping with the exercise of this
complementary movement, after you've
gained entry alongside your partner and
struck him in the biceps as you pulled his
arm to you, pivot back in the opposite
direction and repeat this complementary
movement by dropping your right hand
(immediately after elbow-striking his biceps),
grabbing him at the bend of the elbow, and
pulling him to you as you strike the back of
his arm with a left elbow strike (fig. 40).

From this point in your attack, be
creative and explore other possibilities.
Don't feel limited to striking to the upper
body in this fashion. You can continue

Figure 41   *Figure 42*

pivoting back and forth, pulling with one arm and striking with the other as you crouch lower and lower to encompass elbow strikes to his thigh and back of the knee (figs. 41, 42).

Another application of complementary movement would be to draw your prey in a direction into you to confuse and disorient him as you strike. An example of this would be to step in and to the left of your partner by pulling yourself past him (pulling his right arm with your left hand). This would put a half twist to his upper body that would allow you to reach over and grab the back of his right shoulder with your right hand to pull him to you in order to throw a left elbow strike to his face (figs. 43, 44, 45, 46).

Several things are accomplished with a movement such as this. First of all, you gained entry in such a way as to expose his vulnerable side. You've also positioned yourself behind him and away from his punches and kicks, and you end up putting him into a

Figure 43

Figure 44

Figure 45

Figure 46

partial spin to keep him off balance while you finish out your attack. And once again, take the thrust of this entry and attack and build on it yourself so that you'll end up with an entry and a controlling complementary movement that will harmonize with whatever strike you choose to make.

Figure 47

Figure 48

In times where you might feel compelled
to intervene in violence about to happen to
another, you can effectively utilize complementary movement by approaching your
prey from behind (fig. 47) and stomping to
the back of the knee while you grab the hair
at the top of his head to lever him back and
down onto his knee (fig. 48).

You can also approach someone from an
oblique angle to grip one of his arms at the
shoulder while you reach around to grab the
hair at the side of his head. Then you can twist
and lever him down to the floor, where you
can place your knee atop the back of the neck
to keep him in place (figs. 49, 50, 51, 52).

You can also utilize your prey's clothing
to your advantage while using complementary movement by gripping your hand inside
his belt and pulling him to you as you grip
his throat with your other hand to push him
backward (fig. 53). You can do something
like this to gain control or use it to drive
your prey into an object to injure or stun
him (fig. 54).

There are more ways to utilize this
concept of controlling and injuring your prey
than you might think of in the time it takes
to practice what I've shared with you here.
But I encourage you to put yourself to the
task of discovering more. As you discover
more ways to apply this principle, you'll also
be getting a better feel for controlling your
prey in movement and confining his mobility
through pain and injury.

Seizing your prey in the instant you
decide he is to become prey will put you in
best position to neutralize him before your
confrontation turns into a slugfest. *You–are–
the–predator!* You never want an encounter

Figure 49

Figure 50

Figure 51

Figure 52

Figure 53

Figure 54

with prey to become anything more than what you're best equipped to deal with. You do not want to exchange blows, you do not want to match his speed, and you do not want a contest of strength. It is your prey that brought you to the decision—in whatever way, time, and fashion it took you to make that decision—that he is to be your victim. So, accept what you are and do what you must.

When viewed objectively, weapons are a lot like money. Universally recognized currency is merely a symbol of potential and possibility. We recognize and accept that a twenty dollar bill has a certain value to it, and it's what the twenty dollar bill *represents* rather than what it *is* that gets us what we want.

When you look at a pistol, knife, or club in someone's hand, you have a universal recognition of a symbol of violence that is taken at face value in any nation on Earth for its respective potential and possibilities for pain, injury, or death. So, when you present your twenty dollar bill to a grocer to get something you want, there's a recognition response that takes place within him that tells him it's okay to give it to you, and you can note a look of simple acceptance on his face. If you approach someone who aims a pistol at you, your prey will note the same look of acceptance on *your* face.

Your prey can be calm and confident whether he's robbing you or the grocer with his pistol, because he knows that you will recognize what the clear and present danger is and give him your money. But what your prey doesn't know yet is that *you* are the clear and present danger to *him*.

You're the clear and present danger because you'll have knowledge of movement and fighting skills that your prey isn't likely to have. And because he expects your immediate acceptance of whatever weapon he brandishes, he'll be under the *momentary* belief he has power over you. As a predator, you'll seize the *moment* quickly enough and harshly enough that he won't be able to adjust his focus of attention quickly enough to prevent his fate.

A predator is never far from a weapon. Because a predator initiates the attack, he can use ordinary items to injure his prey when he initiates the attack. Some of these items were discussed in *Sudden Violence,* but as you'll soon see, you'll be using them a little differently in a predatory mode. But for the moment, let's take a look at some potentials and possibilities.

Look at that guy across the street. He looks tired, as though he's trudging home from work where everyone yelled and bitched the life out of him. He bought a newspaper two blocks back that he's carrying tucked under his arm; his other hand is holding a light briefcase.

He looks up in time to see those two characters leaning against the building between him and the bus stop, and he slows his pace even more in hopes they'll simply vanish if he just doesn't look at them. He hangs his head and looks at the ground and then at the shiny brass belt buckle on his new leather belt and tries to look absorbed in thought.

He doesn't want to appear afraid of them, so he picks up his pace and attempts to smile at them. It doesn't work. They close in on either side of him, and he wishes he had a weapon, any weapon at all, because he realizes they're going to hurt him. You can see the color drain from his face as his head darts back and forth between them, hoping against hope that they'll just take his money and leave him alone. Of course, you and I know he's a goner. He became a statistic the instant he dropped his head and didn't prepare for his prey. The ironic thing about our sad fictitious friend is that he had plenty of weapons on him—and plenty of time to use them.

Before going into the actual nuts and bolts of weapon training, I will say that the man in this scenario had an option not to go any further when he first saw the threat in the two characters against the wall. He could have crossed the street, he could have called for a cab, he could have run at the first hint of trouble, and he could have avoided the encounter in a number of other ways.

This book and this type of training aren't for people who are prone to flee at the first hint of trouble. Going headlong into a place where a violent encounter is possible and even probable is the action of one whose predatory nature is close to the surface. If you were walking with a huge and vicious attack dog, you'd probably feel pretty safe in a violent situation. *Yet you are bigger, heavier, and more versatile in your attack, and potentially more vicious than any dog could ever be!* All you have to do is focus on your prey and loosen the beast within!

You shouldn't have to walk through life with your tail tucked between your legs like a cur, and you don't have to. You have a sacred right not to be victimized by human jackals. And though you may not relish the idea of actually having to hurt someone or take his life, you can take solace in the fact that your prey brought a situation to you that made you bring out the best in yourself. You can take pride in being a predator and having the will to be decisive and swift in your actions, regardless of consequences.

Practically any inanimate object has

potential as a weapon. In the above scenario, the briefcase has a hard surface with hard corners that can be used as a bludgeon. The newspaper can be rolled tightly enough to be used to good effect. The belt and buckle has possibilities, as does any pen or pencil that might be within reach. Let's explore some of these possibilities and build from them.

Attacking with a briefcase accords you a few options. The options will differ slightly when you're dealing with one or more prey. If you're going to attack only one prey (fig. 55), you can ram the front edge into his groin (fig. 56). When he bends at the waist from the blow, you can pull upward quickly to slam the top edge of the briefcase under his chin to snap his head back (fig. 57). Then you can rotate your grip on the briefcase to bring it up horizontally and shove its bottom edge into his throat (fig. 58).

This isn't a rigid lesson. When I suggest a technique to you like the one above, allow yourself room for variation. The effectiveness of anything you do will depend on the suddenness and commitment of your attack. If your prey detected your move before you launched it and either blocked it or wasn't hit as hard as you would have liked, *keep hitting him!* And don't stop hitting him until he's through wiggling or runs away from you.

The attack in Figures 55-58 only serves to illustrate possibilities with your briefcase. Though the technique used to illustrate it can work, be prepared to modify your attack if it's disrupted. Explore your briefcase; think of it as a weapon and familiarize yourself with the corners and edges you can use. Be aware also that the way you move

Figure 55

Figure 56

Figure 57

Figure 58

Figure 59

Figure 60

Figure 61

Figure 62

Figure 63

has a lot to do with how effective it can be.

If your prey tries to block you when you try to hit him in the head or neck with the briefcase, you can drop to a crouch as you spin around and use the edge of the case to hammer the back of his knees or sweep his feet out from under him (not as difficult as it sounds) (figs. 59, 60, 61, 62, 63).

Your briefcase can also be used in conjunction with lead-in or follow-up strikes using kicks, punches, and/or other weapons. For instance, you can strike to your prey's face with the rolled newspaper (figs. 64, 65). When the hands come up to his face in response to the strike, you can crouch low to slam the edge of the case into his kneecaps (fig. 66). This will cause him to drop his head and torso in response, which will give you the opportunity to hammer down to the back of his neck with the

Figure 64

Figure 65

Figure 66

Figure 67

briefcase as you smash up into his face with
your knee (fig. 67).

Jam the flat side of the case into your
prey's face (fig. 68). Regardless of if he tries
to intercept and block it or if you're able to
hit him with it, shin strike to the side of his
knee to buckle him (fig. 69). Then crouch
and hook your case behind his legs and use
the handle to pull and sweep his leg or legs
out from under him (figs. 70, 71). Then
stomp him flat!

That should at least get you started on your
way to finding more creative uses for your
briefcase. As for the other weapons our hap-
less victim had at his disposal, let's look at
some of the possibilities he had with his belt.

It seems that most men wear belts more
for cosmetic than practical reasons. If your
pants won't fall down without a belt to hold
them up, then practice unbuckling and
withdrawing it as quickly as you can.

Having done this, wrap the tag or loose
end around your fist several times so that
roughly half the length of the belt is hanging
loose with the buckle at the end of it. Wrap
it in such a way that it wouldn't be easy for
your prey to snag and snatch it from you
were you to use the entire length of it. You
can utilize the buckle more effectively and
with more control in this manner. Having
the belt wrapped in this manner also gives
you the option of using it to ensnare your
prey at any time before or after you commit
to your attack.

As to the time or opportunity to get the
belt out and wrapped in such a fashion, I'll
leave that to the individual's discretion. As
for the use of it as a striking weapon, you
can better prepare yourself by wrapping a

Figure 68

Figure 69

Figure 70

Figure 71

belt around your fist in the manner I described and then getting a kicking bag or
similar object that you can practice hitting.

It's important to know at the outset that
there's more to hitting someone or something
with a belt buckle than merely flailing away.
You must begin by having a target or targets
in mind that you want to hit. You can strike
to the eyes, nose, mouth, and temple area.

As you prepare to strike, avoid the temptation to draw the belt back before you lash
out. Simply throw your body into it by using
your legs to pivot you in such a way that
you can continue the motion up into your
trunk and then out into your arm.

As you attack, direct other blows in succession by using your legs to pivot back and
forth as you rotate your upper body to unleash
your strike. Strive for some semblance of accu-
racy while doing this movement. Additionally,
concentrate on *not* extending your arm to the
extent that you're reaching to hit your prey,
because when you reach, you expose yourself
to a possible countermovement.

Be creative in your attacks, and vary the
combinations you put together. Try some
uppercuts and follow up with a downward
strike to the top of the head or the bridge of
the nose. If you can, let one strike follow on
the heels of the other in quick succession.
Strive to hit hard, accurately, and often. You
can use other kicks and punches, or strike
with the paper or briefcase to further disrupt
and occupy your prey while you change the
angle or intensity of your attack.

If you live or work in an area where an
attack is a probability, you might consider
carrying a cane or walking stick. And if you
do decide to carry one, be aware that if you

flail at someone with it, there's a good chance he can capture it or wrest it from you and use it against you. Since you obviously don't want to give your prey an advantage like that, begin some exploration into use of a cane in a manner that benefits you the most and assists your prey the least. One good way to start is by using it as a club and striking low to the front or sides of the knees. A blow like this creates pain and injury and gives you an angle of attack that effectively keeps it out of his reach.

One advantage that a cane has over a club or baton is that if you strike with the handle end, you can also use it to hook your prey's feet out from under him after you hit him (figs. 72, 73, 74, 75).

You can use the bottom end of your cane to initiate a jab to your prey's face (fig. 76). A strike like this has merit because not only will it hurt him, it will force him to lean back and away from the blow, whether he can block it or not, giving you ample opportunity to knee him in the pelvic girdle (which will now be tilted toward you; fig. 77) or kick or shin strike him to the side of his knees (fig. 78).

When you deliver a strike with your stick in roundhouse fashion, you'll want to keep the elbow of your striking arm at your side. This will give you a good hard blow and will lessen the chance of your prey disarming you (fig. 79).

If you think about it, there are many objects that can be utilized as weapons, but the primary weapon in being a predator is, of course, being a weapon yourself. When you strike your prey with any single or backup object/weapon, realize that it is *you*

Figure 72

Figure 73

Figure 74

Figure 75

Figure 76

Figure 77

Figure 78

Figure 79

as predator that decides, directs, and implements an inanimate object as an extension of your will.

I f you had to name or label your conscious thought process, you might call it intellect. If you were to label a subconscious action, you might call it instinct. As a predator, it's important to understand both functions so that you might call them by another name.

You can safely say that your intellect is the home of your personality. Your intellect is colored by your personality to such an extent that you make value judgments on people, places, and events, and then you decide what your opinion or course of action will be. Your instinct, on the other hand, is what you may regard as the home of the beast.

So that you won't be confused by this, let's look at a hypothetical situation in which you're driving down a residential street and a ball bounces into the road right in front of you, followed in hot pursuit by a small child. If you allowed the time to assess the situation and let your intellect/personality handle it, you'd determine that the best course of action would be to brake the car or swerve to avoid hitting the child (unless you're a psychopath who lives for just such an opportunity). Of course, my point is that the kid would be a goner by the time you made up your mind what to do. Instinct, home of the inner beast, would simply *act in the moment of its happening!*

When your intellect speaks to you through personality, it becomes a logical thought process. When the inner beast speaks to you through instinct, it's an intuitive process. Of the two, more often than not, you're moved more quickly and more surely by the emotion you feel when your instincts speak than when your intellect speaks.

CALLING UP THE BEAST WITHIN

Before continuing much further with the term "beast within" or references to the "inner beast," you should know that the terminology has no other meaning than what is stated in the text. The titles have absolutely no connection whatsoever with anything to do with the occult or demonic or Satanic lore or rituals. The "beast within" is purely poetic/literary license to describe something indescribable.

The beast within, as you'll find, is simply and extraordinarily a huge wellspring of emotional/physical power that you can at once control to stem panic and unleash in an adrenaline rush focused into violent action. If you train seriously and intensely, you'll find the beast as the beast finds you. Think of it as looking for someone inside a building in the middle of the desert in a heavy fog. How do you find such a person? Let's find out.

The prospect of wandering around a foggy desert, aimlessly searching for something you know you're never going to find, seems hopeless and frustrating. Looking within yourself to call up something you're not even sure you have is close to the same feeling.

However, if you had a map and a compass to help you find the place in the desert, you'd eventually find it because you now would have a direction to go and an approximate distance in which you could expect to find it. When you look for the beast within, you have to begin looking in the right direction, and the distance you go to find it depends on how far and how deep you reach so *the beast can find you.*

As to the direction you can begin to

search for your inner beast, I can tell you now that you won't find it within these pages or at anyone's school in any martial art style anywhere in the world. What you'd find is mine and others' beasts. Now that you know where not to look, I'm going to take this opportunity to sit down with you and see if we can reach an understanding so you can begin your search on a path that you might already be on.

To gain more insight into just what kind of animal you're seeking and where it lives, consider the nature of the beast that's called by many other names.

When you see a marathon runner who enters the last mile and convinces everyone but himself that he's not going to make it, and he makes it anyway, they say he has great spirit, or *stamina*.

When a boxer is beaten, bloody, out of breath, and on his last legs, and you feel certain he won't make it one more round, but he goes the distance instead, they say he has *heart*.

When someone's suffered the loss of several loved ones in rapid succession, and you're certain that one more heartbreak will destroy them, and it doesn't, they say he or she has *strength* or *grace*.

There's an exercise in semantics and belief systems in each of these instances. On the one hand, there are those who would say "the Lord helped them!", and there are those who would argue that "the Lord helps those who help themselves," and a debate ensues over who gets credit for whatever amount of physical or spiritual victory there might have been. And it's amazing the level of passion at which people will argue this point.

However, if someone falls short of his goals, if someone just can't take one more blow or one more step, everyone would be in agreement that the individual was totally and personally responsible for his respective failures.

Before you side with either of these arguments, consider this. In each of the examples above, *they reached deep within themselves for the strength to carry them through!*

They found their strength and resolve in the middle of crisis to see them through the storm. The nature of the beast is such that it thrives on the chaos and pressure we would normally shun. The beast begins to take form and rear its massive head, to flare its nostrils, and to reveal its fangs in the face of fear and uncertainty. But how is it called? Why does it answer one person's call and not another's?

The beast within is no different than an attack dog in that it responds to its name and specific commands it was trained to respond to. The beast within is no farther away than your last heartbeat and is as close as your next breath, and it's called to your side by the conviction of your will. There's a quickening that takes place within you and the beast simultaneously with the determination of the unformed thought, "I'm–going–to–do–this!" The beast will *not* be manifest with the emotional feeling of, "I might not be able to do this."

So, the direction you need to seek the beast is within, and the distance you need to travel is measured in the seeking. Does that sound vague? Then think about expending the pounds of flesh, the pints of sweat, and the ounces of blood you'd invest in an activity such as fighting and sports. The distance you travel is measured in direct proportion to the sacrifices you're willing to make for physical, emotional, and spiritual discipline and stretching to attain your personal best in every aspect of your being.

And when you do this, you'll come to realize a very certain and profound confidence in yourself that fills your every pore and projects to fill the areas of the focus of your attention on every path you travel. When you reach deep within and find you're made of better stuff than you thought, you'll also find yourself on solid footing in crisis situations.

So, you can safely say that the nature of the beast is to protect you. *Some call it self-preservation.*

The home of the beast is in the deepest and darkest corner of your conscience. If you have to ask yourself, "Can I take this man's life? Can I really hurt him?" *then you haven't met the beast yet!*

The distance to the beast is measured in how far you came and how far you're willing to go to find it. If you haven't been in situations where you've had to reach to the bottom of your gut or the top of your soul, then chances are you'll have to make the opportunity to cover the distance. *You* have to make the journey to the beast. The beast won't come to you until you've mastered it and earned its ownership. And while the beast resides in each of us, the difference is in *how much it's been cul-tivated to grow.* In someone who insists on remaining meek and mild and wouldn't consider hurting a fly, the beast in him will be as a tiny puppy. When danger makes its presence known, all the timid will hear is a tiny yap, yap, yap. Whereas in someone who takes the time to learn who he is and grows beyond who he thought he was, *the beast that emerges will be as a grizzly bear!*

We truly are the sum total of every decision we've ever made. And when you decide to feed the beast and make it grow, *it will grow!* When you decide to slumber and live a life of ease and look for someone else to protect you, *the beast will wander away to hibernate.*

You can have a ferocious power in your hands that will protect you always. Decide now to master the beast. Believe now, and it will happen!

There doesn't seem to be a very good reason to seek your prey in the dark. After all, martial art skills are ostensibly used for self-defense, right? You might even ask why you'd want to look for someone in the dark, because it's logical to assume your prey would be seeking you out where he could see you, wouldn't he?

Training in the dark and darkened environs accords you the opportunity to think and train as a predator more completely so that when you're in the neighborhood with lesser trained predators who would devour you, they'll have no idea what they've gotten themselves into. You will. And that's all that matters.

The nature of the beast is such that it's most aware when you're most afraid. I'm talking now about the beast within your prey. If you walk down an alley, darting your head back and forth as though you're going to bolt and run at any instant, the beast within your prey will become increasingly confident that it selected you wisely.

The way you carry yourself, the way you make eye contact, and the way you walk says more about you in a glance than what you might think. If–you–are–afraid, and if you worry you're going to be attacked—somewhere, you just don't quite know where yet—your body will betray your thoughts, no matter how much tough talk you're promising yourself.

So where you might be *thinking,* "Uh huh, I'm baaad. Yep, here comes one badass dude ready to whip ass on the first sucker that looks at me wrong!" your body will be *saying,* "I'm going to soil my pants aaany minute now. Yep, may even wet 'em too."

NIGHT STALKING

And where your prey might have been undecided at first whether to ignore you or give you a hard time, your body English tells him it's quite alright to take you off because, hell, you don't even know what you came here for anyway.

So how do we turn this around and give you the self-confidence to project the power and potential of the beast within you? So that when you look at them and smile, what the beast within them will hear is, "Yeah, you'll make a nice snack. Come closer and I'll tear a chunk outta your ass."

Quiet confidence is a real confidence. It's an attitude that says to your prey, "I'll take your life before you can take my confidence." Your prey will believe it, because it will be true.

Now, to build a base for you to grow on, I'm going to take you into darkened alleyways and corridors. I'm going to involve you in the planning and execution of an ambush, and I'm going to lead you into an ambush to be attacked. I'm going to draw you into a trap of up to four other predators, and I'm going to equip you with some tools to get away from them and draw them into your own ambush as you are pursued. I'm going to frustrate you, exhaust you, and surprise you.

First of all, in order to give you some exposure to darkened environments and some familiarity with working in the dark, I'm going to have you invite four or five of your friends or family who will commit to seeing this section through. I realize that may be a pretty tough job all by itself, but it's important to have some people who will take this seriously.

If you have such a group ready and are

willing to begin, then let's begin. I'm going
to bring you to a room of your choosing,
but a room that will be pitch black. When
you have such a room, it will be time to
practice a little body and darkness
orientation exercise.

Before you turn the lights out, situate
yourself in the middle of the room. If the
room isn't perfectly black when you do
this, then supplement the darkness by
adding a blindfold.

Have your partners, one at a time, make
their way across the room as best they can
and try to locate you by feel. Once they
touch you, simply have them hold onto you
for a few moments while you orient yourself
to their touch and your relation to the rest of
their body.

Notice first the pressure of their fingers
and the location of their thumbs (this is a
training exercise, and you're allowed as
much time as it takes). Feel which is the
right or left hand, and that will tell you what
areas your partner has exposed to you.

If your partner touches/grabs your arm,
concentrate on the pressure of the thumb
and work backward from there so that if
you clamp one hand over his to lock it in
place, you'll know that by pivoting in one
direction you're going to feel the bend of
the elbow. Or you can lock the elbow and
arm out in the other and figure from there
whether you'll touch the front of his body or
the back. Continue on so you'll know
whether you can possibly deliver a shin
strike to the front, sides, or backs of the
knees, *all because of the feel of the grip of
your partner's hand.*

From there, take a few moments to feel

with your hands the distance and position of your partner's body surfaces in relation to yours. With one of your hands still placed atop your partner's hand, gauge the distance between you so you'll know whether punches and kicks or knee and elbow strikes are in order.

You'll still have the option to initiate a wrist leverage in any case, but you'll still benefit from knowing which way you can torque your partner/prey so you can know whether he's going to end up on his back, belly, or knees.

After you've all had a few turns at this and can readily determine distance, angle, and body target relationship, you can move on to the next phase—stalking your prey in the dark.

The problems for you to solve will be in locating, capturing, and neutralizing your prey on contact. And to give yourself an advantage, you'll want to be in optimum position yourself when you find your prey.

When most students are put to the test to see how they would seek someone out in total darkness, with very few exceptions they'll grope around with their arms out-stretched and shuffle slowly in the direction in which they think they're going to find something. If the student were to be looking for the light switch, this would be alright. But for our intent and purpose, it's not alright. The principal difference between how most people would move in the dark and how a predator searches the dark is attitude.

As you seek out your partner in this exercise, the important thing for you to remember is that you aren't trying to *find* your partner; you are seeking *to capture your prey!* In order to best serve your purpose, you need to be in a body position that will provide you balance in movement, both in stepping and reaching. And you'll want to cut as wide a swath in the dark as you safely can without dangerously overextending yourself.

You can begin by settling your weight in a mid to low comfortable crouch, with your first step being forward and to the right at a 45-degree angle. As you do this, position your arms at mid-chest level, as though you've drawn back a bow. Have your palms facing forward. Your right arm should be bent at the elbow and your left arm extended, but not all the way. And don't reach any farther away from you than the end of your leading foot (fig. 80).

Figure 80

Take as long a step as you normally do and sweep your arms in a path to the right as you step with the right foot. Stepping and moving your arms in this manner does several things to help you catch your prey. By not exaggerating your steps and crouching slightly, you'll be in a well-balanced posture in which you can move quickly and easily. By stepping forward and to the right and left at 45-degree angles, you'll be cutting a wider swath in the darkness than you'd normally be able to. And with your arms held in the position described, you'll be able to feel your way in the dark and locate your prey in an easy sweeping motion. When you locate him, your limbs will be in good position to capture him.

You must remember as you do this, though, that until you and he get together in the dark, he'll be aware you're looking for him and will be in a defensive mode to prepare himself if and when he's caught by you. Because of this, he may try to grab you and pull you down. This is why you don't want to overextend your reach with your arms when you're sweeping and feeling for him. If your arms are too far forward, it will be a relatively easy matter for your prey to grab your arm and pull you off balance.

As you step in this exercise, move your feet in such a way that you're not taking tall steps but rather sweeping in front of you along with your arms. The reason for this is the possibility of stepping on a bottle, can, marble, or anything else that will betray your presence and position and possibly cause you to slip and fall.

Now practice this movement awhile, but

don't get so fixated on the movement that you move stiffly and mechanically. Try to get into a slow but steady rhythm that will allow you to cover plenty of space in a short amount of time (much like roller skating). Do this before you actually seek your partner/prey in the darkness.

After you've been in the position of both predator and prey in this exercise and feel comfortable enough to expand the exercise a little, you can now practice what you might want to do to your prey once you've found him. For this, let's practice a few techniques that are relatively easy to execute.

The optimum technique will have your prey in your control in the first seconds of contact. If you lash out with kicks and punches when you feel close enough to your prey to do so, you'll either miss and betray your presence or knock him away from you and have to seek him out again. By striking out and losing control of your initial contact, you'll increase the difficulty of your next contact because he'll be punching and kicking at the nearest sound and movement and possibly hitting you.

So when you first make contact, concentrate on techniques that will only serve to gather your prey in and smother any movement he might make. Think of it as being like a boa constrictor; the huge snake doesn't squeeze its prey to death but rather tightens up on it any time it moves until it's suffocated.

As you feel for your prey and touch his arm, chest, or back, swiftly slide your hand up to his neck and head to gain immediate control. Utilize his chin, hair, neck, and shoulders to effect a standing neck break and/or a takedown. Make your takedown happen quickly *(being extremely careful with your partner!)* by dropping to one or both knees (figs. 81, 82, 83).

If you suspect your prey might be armed with a knife or a club, and it's imperative that you stalk and neutralize him, you can do so by lowering your body closer to the ground. Stalking from a three-point base gives you a better position to approach your prey in the event he takes a swipe at you if he senses you near.

To adopt a three-point base to begin stalking him, you'll need to move and sweep your arms in the same fashion as you do when you're upright. The only difference is that instead of walking in a crouch, you'll move from one knee to the other.

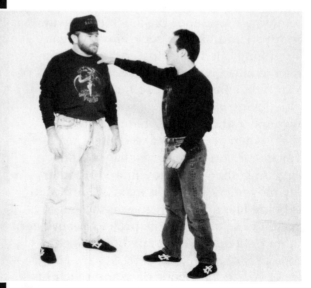

Figure 81

Figure 82

Figure 83

Figure 84

As you do this, you'll initially set yourself to the floor onto one knee. We'll start by stepping forward as you normally would in this exercise, but you'll be settling your weight onto your left knee and the ball of your left foot (fig. 84). The three-point base position is comprised of contact areas of the right foot, left knee, and left foot in this example.

You can begin to move across the room in this fashion, making as smooth a transition from one step to the next as you can.

When you make contact with your prey from the floor, you can deliver a forearm hammer strike to the back or front of his knee or knees, or you can sweep his legs from under him to drop him onto the floor (figs. 85, 86, 87).

Figure 85

Figure 86

Figure 87

Once your prey is down, you need to keep in mind that he will probably still have the knife or club in his hand, and he might not be injured badly enough to prevent him from trying to hit you as soon as he hits the floor. This being the case, the most prudent course of action for you to take would be to avoid his upper body and concentrate your attack to stomps and kicks to his legs and twisting his foot to break the ankle if it's accessible (figs. 88, 89). You should effect your attacks upon your prey *immediately* upon hitting the floor. Use his legs or ankles to rotate his body so that he's on his belly to reduce the range of his abilities to use his weapon. Be fast and be violent!

Practice this exercise both upright and from the three-point base enough so that you're completely comfortable with it. Take the time to assess your situation and problem-solve your way through it. Take extreme care when practicing neck-break takedowns and knee strikes. Feel where his limbs and vital areas are so that you can concentrate your attention and attacks on the areas that you can do the most damage to in the least amount of time.

Once you thoroughly familiarize yourself with this mode of training, I want you to remember it and return to it from time to time as your predation training progresses.

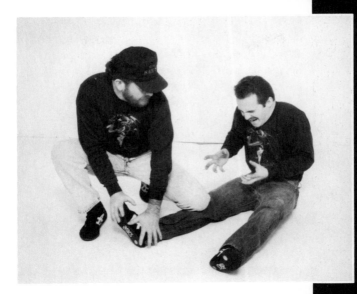

Figure 88

Figure 89

Befefore you begin this chapter, I want to share a few words with you about training from a book. It's important that you read and understand this now before you continue any further, because your training will be more demanding and your resolve will begin to weaken unless you fully believe in what you're doing.

I'm going to instruct, direct, and try to help you to become more than you might have thought you could be, but in order for this to happen, you need to *participate* wholeheartedly in your training. As you throw yourself bodily into this task, you'll end up reading these pages and doing what the instructions require of you.

Some will say that you can't learn from a book, and some will say it's foolish to even try. Do you believe this? Even though you're reading the pages of this book with the certain knowledge that it was some time in the past that it was written, submitted for publication, printed, and distributed to the place where you ordered it or bought it from, you'd never guess that on a cosmic level, I'm here as you read this. Weird isn't it? The sound you hear within your head as you read this to yourself is partially my own voice directing your attention and focus of thought, through your own thought voice!

It's only through books that you were able to learn anything in school. There was a teacher present to tell you what to read, how much to read, when to read it, and to write a report and take tests on what you read to prove you read and understood it.

This whole process was necessary because the things you read were *required reading*. And since studying these various

TACKLING PREY

subjects were mandatory to pass your classes and move up in grade levels, the importance of reading was lost for the most part because it was an inconvenience. There were much more fun and important things to do than sit around reading books.

While you're thinking about this, give some thought to what you used to think a book was and what it represents to you now. Before, a book represented homework and grades, something you had to plod through to get what you needed out of it. Now, by reading a book of your own choosing, it represents potential with a prize inside!

If you know how to read, and if you can *understand* what you've read, *you can learn and understand anything!* Think about that for a moment: *you–can–learn–anything!* The only conflict you can get from this is the application of what you read, and ideally that's what teachers are for. Teachers can bring you from *understanding* a subject to the *realization* of your knowledge.

Understanding and realizing something is like being in the back seat of a car and watching someone start it up and drive. If you've never driven before, and if you watch closely enough, you can *understand* how a car is driven. It's when you get behind the wheel yourself and actually drive the car that you then *realize* how to drive.

So by selecting a book like this one to read, you've done more than you might be aware of as far as learning is concerned. First of all, you're interested enough in the subject matter to buy it. You're therefore motivated enough to read it (because you *want* to, not because you have to). You can read as much as you want, when you want, as many times as you want, without someone putting limitations on just how much you should read, *because it's your own idea to do it*.

From a teaching perspective, you're in better position to learn about predator training by reading this book than you would be if we were to meet and I were to teach you personally. Why? Because if you and I were to meet, I'd only be able to discuss specific issues as you asked about them or as I brought them up. By reading this book, or any other book by anyone else on any other topic, you're able to have in your hands, from cover to cover, more information about what you're interested in, covered more thoroughly and pragmatically, than if you were to spend a long time with the author of the book.

Therefore, by buying this book, you've set into motion the mental, physical, and philosophical process needed to awaken the beast within you and become the predator you already are *but don't know it*.

By reading the principles and techniques within the book, you'll *understand* the value in the training. And by doing the physical things required of you as you work your way through this book, you'll *realize* the presence of who you really are by the confidence you'll gain in discovering you were a giant all along. Sort of like a circus bear that has the innate ability to make hamburger of its trainer, but it just never occurs to it that it can.

So, without further delay, let's get back to some more training. I'm going to show you and your partners another facet of predator/prey training that might make you rethink what your idea of a predator is. So far, you'd be right in assuming that a predator is always on the attack. However, I'm going to show you ways and means of a predator in retreat laying ambush to prey in pursuit. The instance in which this might happen is when the "prey harvest" is greater than the ability of the predator.

To begin, you and your partners need to go to a grassy area, a wrestling room, or a thick-carpeted area. I'm going to have each of you in turn practice tackling the designated predator. The people doing the tackling will need to make a committed effort to take down the predator and protect themselves when going to the ground if they're shrugged off.

It is important to understand the dynamics of a tackle before you begin to try to deflect, ward off, or struggle with your tackling prey. The idea of a tackle is to suddenly build enough momentum to bowl you over as the arms wrap around and contain you as you go to the ground. Ordinarily, this turns into a grappling match once you're on the ground. Since you're going to be dealing with multiple prey in this area of training, you won't have the time to fight your way out of it before the rest of the prey pounces on you.

A natural temptation would be to try to confront a tackle by delivering a kick, knee strike, or punch to the tackler as he arrives. The danger in this is that the momentum of the tackle will knock you off balance and onto your butt. Since we don't want this to happen, let's get one of your partners in front of you and frozen in the position of an attempted tackle.

Most tackles will take place at waist level,

with the arms spread wide enough apart to get around you. Very often, the person doing the tackling will try to drive you into and pin you against a wall. This is usually a good play because there's good opportunity to stun and injure you.

Have your partner stand before you at waist level with his arms about to wrap around you. Have him pause there a few moments while you assess his position and yours.

If you charge into him, you'll be using force against force, which won't serve you well at all (fig. 90). If you turned to leave and tried to distance yourself from him, you'd simply be tackled from behind (fig. 91). But if you drop one leg back so that your shoulders aren't square with his but rather are sideways to him, the force and drive of his tackle will be deflected alongside instead of into you (fig. 92).

Figure 90

Figure 91

Figure 92

Since the key element of a successful
tackle is a sudden and committed charge,
you'll want to time your movement to
correspond to his. In order to do that, I have
a short drill for you to practice before you
attempt to handle a tackle effectively.

Have one of your partners get about 8
feet away and go into a partial crouch, as
though to rush you. You'll be facing him,
and the idea is to time your turning point to
your partner's arrival. Have your partner
charge toward *and alongside* you rather
than into you. You should simply pivot in
his direction and run with him so that you're
shoulder to shoulder when he comes even
with you.

For instance, if your partner charges at
you to your left, turn to your left by dropping back your left leg and rotating into him
to have your right shoulder pressed to his
left shoulder. Now run with him for a few
short steps (figs. 93, 94, 95, 96). This exercise should provide you with the timing
necessary to deflect a tackle.

To utilize this drill to perform the actual
tackle deflection, you'll need to drop back
with your left leg as you reach up under his
armpit with your right arm to further direct
him around you (figs. 97, 98, 99, 100, 101).

You will need to make a smooth body
shift so that you turn sideways by dropping
back your left leg *as* you reach under his
arm with yours to direct him around you.
Try very hard not to grab him with your
other arm too, because this will cause you
to be caught and tackled. Of course, you
can use either leg to drop back, as long as
you use the opposite arm to guide your
prey around you.

Figure 93

Figure 94

Figure 95

Figure 96

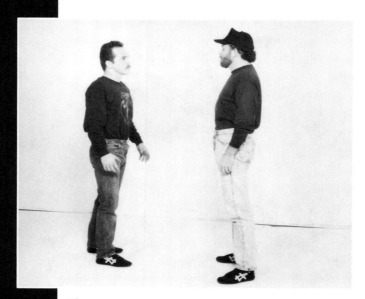

Figure 97

Figure 98

Figure 99

Figure 100

Figure 101

Should you be tackled from behind and become aware of it in time to do something about it, you can make a variation of this movement skill.

Have your partner poise himself behind you and take a moment to take stock of your situation (fig. 102). What you'll need to do once you feel him move in is step forward with your right foot as you bring your left arm up under his to direct him past you (figs. 103, 104). This position will present you full front to him, but he'll still be directed past. If you can act quickly enough, it would benefit you to take another step back (to continue your prey's direction) as you hook under his arm (figs. 105, 106). It isn't essential to do this, but it will be helpful.

Figure 102

These techniques for tackle deflection
are, of course, textbook examples in best-
case scenarios in a controlled environment.
But this is where you learn a movement skill
that may pay huge dividends in time and
safety during a rush of prey. Still, by your
partners actually trying to bring you down,
you're going to find a fast but natural
rhythm to address and deflect a tackle.

Very shortly, I'm going to be involving
you in multiple attack scenarios where
tackling will play a big role, and they will
come at a time when you won't be prepared
for them. This will tell you if you need to
spend more time practicing these skills. But
for now, set this book down and go back to
work. For the direction in which I'm going
to be taking you, you'll need it.

Figure 103

Figure 104

Figure 105

Figure 106

I t starts out harmlessly enough. You leave the theater and head to your car parked a couple blocks away. It's nice out, it was a nice movie you watched while you waited for your girlfriend to get home from work, and the steamy action midway through the film left you feeling a little rowdy.

Walking with a little bounce to your step, you think about the star-quality moves you're going to put on her, and how she's just going to be on fire with passion, and boy oh boy aren't we going to have a big time tonight. You notice a shortcut behind a building that'll get you to your car sooner, and you think nothing of strolling down that darkened alleyway. There's nothing to fear, because you're a trained and accomplished martial artist, a fighter whose skill is only exceeded by your readiness to take on all comers.

It's really dark in the alley, but a car just turned on its headlights. While it's light now, and you can see things in your peripheral vision, the dark corners and the areas around the headlights aren't visible at all. Not to worry, though, you can see a couple of guys lounging around next to the building and you can take them easily enough. If that guy in the car would just dim those damn headlights, you could see the rest of the alleyway and anyone else there.

There's a sudden movement to your right and you turn to face it. It's a man charging toward you with what looks like a short club. You deftly move aside as you power a kick to his nearest knee. The kick never arrives because as you focused on delivering it, you were grabbed from behind and nearly toppled.

CHAP 12

AMBUSHES

125

Your senses are radiantly alive and alert. You can hear these guys grunt as they crush you between them. You can hear the sounds of several feet slapping against the pavement getting louder as they close in on you too. And you can hear the sound of your heartbeat loudest of all. It came with the copper taste of fear when you realized you were trapped with your arms pinned at your sides.

You kick in one direction, headbutt the guy behind you, and stomp on someone else's foot as you try desperately to break free. But every time you try to launch a punch or kick, someone grabs it, and you're compressed tighter and tighter in the middle of them. You're now taking punches and kicks that you're unable to block or avoid. These blows have stunning impact that make your ears ring, your groin ache, your chest heave, and your eyes water. And it doesn't let up!

All the sound has been drowned out by the screams of rage of the beast within. You wrench this way and that; you bite this guy as you knee that one. But you feel like a lion in a cage being tormented by vicious fools. You know you have the power and the ability to destroy these prey, and your fury knows no bounds as you spend every ounce of your spirit on just trying to get away and get some room to fight, to teach these guys what pain is all about.

But the sad truth of it is, you–are–trapped! Like the lion in the cage, your ferocity is all that keeps you conscious as you're beaten to the ground and stomped. On the way to the ground, you dive and roll out from among them and take off running.

You're dizzy and your vision is impaired by all the blood running into your eyes.

You're still in better shape than most of these guys, so you run like you've never run before. You can feel the bitter sensation of bile come to your throat and the chill of ice water pour into the pit of your stomach as panic sets in.

As you run through the open area of the parking lot, they begin to catch up and surround you. You try to fight them off again, deciding to take lives if you can. The sudden stress of fighting and running has you panting like a dog. Through your eyes you see an equal mixture of blood and tears. You feel more helpless at this moment than at any other in your life. Blows are hammering you everywhere, and within seconds you are beaten senseless.

You awake in a hospital in more pain than you ever thought humanly possible. A doctor tells you that with therapy, you might be able to walk again. Walk again? How the hell could this happen to you? You're an exceptional martial artist. *This isn't supposed to happen!*

I agree, it isn't supposed to happen. If you spend a large portion of your time in a martial arts school and invest the time and energy necessary to become a fighter, you shouldn't have to worry about the above scenario happening to you.

My point in involving you is to point out that there is an enormous difference between thinking like a martial artist and thinking like a *predator* martial artist. The difference is important, and I'll show you why.

As martial artists, we're led by ego and confidence in our training and ability, so when we see people we feel comfortable about beating in a fight, we won't balk at the prospect of engaging in a fight. As *predator* martial artists, we operate on instinct and logic.

Our instinct at the entrance to the alleyway would have detoured us back to the sidewalk. Why? Because entering the alley posed too many unknown elements. With the headlights in our eyes, we can't determine if there are two or twenty prey. And while we aren't reluctant to attack our prey, we choose to do it in our section of the jungle, not theirs.

But this part of your training will better enable you to escape the trap your prey will lay for you and run them instead through your own gauntlet of traps in your flight away from them. And yes, that's right, predators sometimes run. The principal difference between running ahead of our prey and running from our prey will become apparent as we delve more thoroughly into it in this chapter.

For now, though, let's return to that alley. Gather your training partners around and try a simple exercise before you get hot and heavy into the actual training.

Find an alley where there's no escape route other than the entrance or exit. Have three of your partners situate themselves somewhere in the alley where they can ambush you without your knowing their immediate whereabouts. When they've hidden or situated themselves, have them call out to you.

You will enter the alley with the expectation of leaving through the other end. At some point, they should try to rush and capture you. There should be no attack other than to grab and hold you. All you should attempt to do is simply get away. Don't try to punch or kick just yet; just try to get away and run from them.

When you're sufficiently trapped and immobile, it will be time to stop and trade positions so that you are one of the ambushers. You should each take a turn in planning the ambush and each take a turn in trying to escape the ambush. Do this now.

For obvious reasons, there is value in planning an ambush. It allows you to view the environment as a variety of places to conceal yourself and your partners and lay in waiting to launch a surprise attack. You begin to think like a pack predator in planning the doom of prey who don't even know you exist yet.

So from this aspect of the training, look at the entrance to an alleyway, darkened parking garage, or any other place that invites an ambush, and think about how you might plan an ambush against yourself. See where the shadows are darkest, what offers the best concealment, where other escape routes can best be cut off, etc.

It's important that you view these places in such a way because once you enter them, *you're committed!* You accept the situation and become hyperalert as you move through the area to where you're going. *But you still have the option not to enter.*

Back to the training again. You will have discovered by now how very easy it is to be captured and wrestled to the ground, no matter how valiantly you resist. There's a reason for this. When you struggle against those who would wrestle you to the ground, there's a natural tendency to resist by bracing yourself with your legs to push, pull, and shove against these people in order to create an opening for you to escape. But when you do this, you're giving your prey something to grab onto and hold you with. By bracing and shoving with your legs, you're limiting your own mobility, which further ensures your capture.

What I'm going to have you do now is practice a movement skill. It may look silly to you, and I know already that when you do it you'll complain about it feeling unnatural. But before you purse your lips and suggest that I practice an unnatural act upon myself, I want you to think about a few things.

If you're dropped for whatever reason into a deep pool of water, the *natural* thing to do is begin to flail your arms wildly and struggle to stay afloat *even as you drown*. The *trained response* would be to swim. And while swimming may correctly be regarded as an unnatural act, it is an unnatural act that will save your life!

Driving a car, flying a plane, operating a lawnmower, performing open-heart surgery, figure skating, flying a kite, knitting, sewing, operating a television and VCR, riding a horse, and playing golf all are unnatural acts. And when you attempt to try these or countless other tasks that you take for granted, remember, they were all unnatural at first. When you apply yourself to the task, however, you will accomplish it. When you become proficient at it, people will say you are *a natural*. Ironic isn't it?

So, let's get you and your partners grouped together again, and bring this book to the corridor you have selected. Have two or three of your partners approach with the intent to capture you. You'll assume there's a wall behind you to prevent your escape, so you can focus your attention on getting past your partners.

If you charge in-between two of them, they'll be able to utilize four arms between them to capture you. If you make your escape between the wall and one of them, you'll only be contending with two arms. As you make your dash between your partner and the wall, you will want to keep your arms pressed to your chest, with fingertips under your chin. You'll also be keeping your legs close together and rotating in a tight and fast pirouette in the direction of your partner as you move alongside the wall (figs. 107, 108, 109, 110).

The direction you rotate is important. If you look down the corridor and the wall is to your left, then you should spin clockwise. If you were to spin counterclockwise, you'd probably find yourself winding into the enveloping arms of your partner (figs. 111, 112, 113).

In the beginning, it's not uncommon to find yourself getting dizzy as you tight-spin through your partner/prey. Ideally, you'll project yourself in the direction of the end of the corridor, focusing on this to keep your equilibrium.

You'll still find yourself getting caught as you do this because you're going to struggle when your partner grabs you. You're going to plant your feet and twist this way and that, probably cuss a lot, but that's okay. It's part of the process. You need to know where you're failing so you can proceed to success.

The principal reason you'll get caught

Figure 107

Figure 108

Figure 109

Figure 110

Figure 111

Figure 112

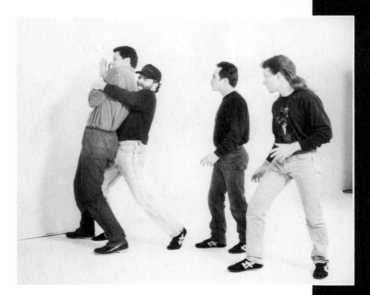

Figure 113

when you plant your feet is this: you won't
be able to spin out of a stationary position
where your legs are wider apart than your
shoulders (figs. 114, 115, 116).

You will want to time your exit to a point
where they're very nearly upon you. This
way you can burst between the wall and
your prey. If you charge directly at the slot,
they'll simply bunch up and intercept you.
And while the spinning movement skill
might get you past them, it has a greater
chance of failure if you give them an
indication of what you're about to do.

So, when they're walking toward you,
remain still or walk toward them too. But at
the moment you close with them, make
your escape! Be quick and decisive about it.

Keeping your arms in front of you with
your hands under your chin is important to
keep in mind as you execute this spinning

Figure 14

Figure 115

Figure 116

escape movement skill. The reason for this
is that if your arms are outstretched, you'll
get caught. If your forearms are held below
the level of your elbows, it's easy to get
caught around the waist and have your arms
trapped (fig. 117).

However, if you keep your arms up to
your chin, you'll have some leverage to
press your arms out of such a grab. And
with your arms near your head and chest,
you'll be able to ward off blows directed at
you without committing to a returning
volley and exposing your limbs to possible
capture (fig. 118).

Once you've made good your escape,
you'll need to orchestrate your own
"running ambush." It's important for you to
know at the beginning that if you have
several prey hot on your trail, your chances
of survival are better if you deal with them

Figure 117

Figure 118

along the way rather than hoping against hope you can outrun them. Wild dogs are able to run deer to the ground by their persistence rather than speed. If you give an all-out burst of speed to get away from them, you will be completely and entirely exhausted by the time your prey catches up to you and in no condition to hurt them.

You should pace yourself so that you're far enough ahead of them that they pose no immediate danger (if time, speed, and distance permit). Run if you can to the side of a building or alongside parked cars close enough that you can almost feel the building brush your skin (fig. 119). You do this so that you can focus your attention 180 degrees to the front and behind you, and run them into solid objects as they come up.

Figure 119

If you run directly to an open space, your prey will be able to surround you, and your focus of attention will have to encompass 360 degrees. If you have to look side-to-side and front-to-back as you're running full tilt, there remains a high risk of running directly into an object as you run (figs. 120, 121). *This is unacceptable!*

If your prey is surrounding you as you run, your perspective of the situation will change from "leading your prey through a gauntlet of collision objects" to "running for survival." In the blink of an eye and a gasp of air, your status will change from predator to prey.

And so, in order to lay waste to your prey in pursuit of you, you will need to practice a couple of movement skills with your partners. Have them trot behind you as you jog alongside a fence or wall. Have a big cardboard box placed well ahead of you for something to direct your prey into. You will, of course, slam dunk your partner/prey into the box as you get to it.

You will want to adjust your pace so that you and your partner arrive at the box at the same time, in much the same way as you would strike a baseball with a bat—you'd hit the ball as it arrives rather than before it gets to you or after it gets past you.

And to better facilitate the movement skill to be able to run, pivot and slam, and continue to run without breaking stride, you'll need to try a running exercise. Have your partner jog after you as you adjust the pace to arrive even with the box at the same time.

The person chasing you only has the responsibility of catching you. It's *your* job to speed up or slow down enough to en-

Figure 120

Figure 121

sure that you arrive at the box at the same time. Keep doing this until you are both consistently arriving at the box at the same time. Do this now.

Once you're able to accomplish this, have your partner again chase after you. This time as you arrive at the box, pivot 180 degrees to face him *while you're still running*. You'll be running backward, but that's the point of the exercise.

You should be able to lead your prey to the box and pivot around to face him while still running without breaking your stride. Once you're able to accomplish this, you will want to pivot around again so that you're running forward.

If you are able to run, pivot and run backward, and pivot and run forward again fairly easy, try doing it in fewer steps until you can finally narrow it down to three. You should end up being able to step forward, step-pivot backward, and step-pivot forward without breaking stride (figs. 122, 123, 124, 125).

Once this movement is accomplished, you'll need to rotate in a manner that gives you the best line and angle of attack to drive your partner into the box easily. To do this, position yourself alongside a wall to your left side. The direction of rotation is the same as the body spin discussed earlier.

Since you'll want to direct your prey into the wall itself or an object next to the wall, you'll need to rotate away from it so that when you complete the rotation, you'll be driving them into the wall. Simplified: if the wall is to your left, rotate to the right; if the wall is to your right, rotate to the left (figs. 126, 127, 128, 129).

As you rotate and drive your

Figure 122

Figure 123

Figure 124

Figure 125

Figure 126

Figure 127

Figure 128

partner/prey into the wall or the object
against the wall, try to make as little
separation from the wall as you can. If you
get a body's width of separation from the

Figure 129

wall, it will provide another prey the opportunity to get past you on that side and effectively have you surrounded.

Spend more than what you might think to be an inordinate amount of time practicing these movement skills. They are simple and effective once you have them mastered, and the understanding and application will accord you a greater measure of confidence. And as grows your confidence, *so grows the beast!*

CHAP 13

PREDATOR ETHICS

An issue that's frequently raised and seldom addressed is how one should conduct oneself when pressed into horseplay. This is such a subjective matter that anyone would be hard-pressed to give a definitive answer. Still, I'm compelled to offer some food for thought because there are enough instances where you can be baited into unleashing the beast unnecessarily.

The first thing you might ask yourself before you give the beast room to roam is how well you like or dislike the person who initiates the horseplay. Then you should have a standard of what constitutes friendly horseplay or thinly veiled acts of "sneak violence." Decide how much and how far you're willing to let someone go in his horseplay.

The physical aspects of it can run the gamut of pushing, pinching, grabbing, tackling, headlocking, hair grabbing, slapping, and wrestling. The degree and intensity will again determine what you should say or do.

Once horseplay's been initiated, you need to decide how important this event is to you. Can you ignore it? Should you jump in his face about it? Should you grapple with him until you "win"? Should you just beat the crap out of him as an example? Can you effectively tell him you don't want to engage in it? Of course, you can do anything you want. But the net result of the way you handle it will have consequences, both immediate and long-range.

Friend and enemy alike share a common thought when they engage you in rough-house activities. If they know you to be a martial artist, they will expect some degree of restraint on your part.

Should you exercise restraint? Should you be expected to suffer slapstick indignities because the people you're around think it's fun? Or should you simply ignore the whole process and give them the opportunity to chill out?

There are still too many variables to give a definite answer one way or the other. However, before you plan a course of action the next time you're pressed into horseplay, consider some subsurface issues that ride with your decision.

First of all, just because someone is an adult doesn't necessarily mean he's mature. And because he lacks maturity, he also lacks the understanding that you don't place as high a degree of fun in the horseplay as he does. If he's your friend, and he knows you're a martial artist, he will take a certain measure of pride in himself that he can rough you up and get away with it because you're "pals." *He trusts you not to harm him.* And of course if you do hurt him, even if it's something as simple as knocking the wind out of him or slam dunking him, all in fun, mind you, *he'll feel disappointed and betrayed by you!*

If you've ever had a puppy that wanted to play by growling and chewing on your foot or pant leg, and you ignored it, it grew bored and went on to something else. If you briskly rub its head back and forth, it signals to the pup your willingness to play, *and it will never leave you alone!*

Still, you can imagine the hurt look you'd get from the pup if you were to reach out with your foot and just kick the ass right off of it. So again, what's the appropriate course of action? Again, it depends mostly upon how much value you place on the individual involving you in the horseplay.

If you like the person or persons a lot, and he or they grab you in a bear hug and pick you up, you can simply shrug the incident off by saying in a patronizing tone, "Okay, you've got me. Now put me down." At this point you can tell them forthright and honestly that you feel manhandling someone in that way is embarrassing and demeaning. *That's why you don't play grab-ass with them like that!* You tell them that you realize they mean no harm, and you can understand their fun with it, but what they're doing is beginning to annoy you, and you don't want to think badly of them because you value their friendship.

If your friends ignore an honest statement like that and still want to roughhouse with you, then believe it, *they aren't your friends!* Quickly and efficiently let the beast out far enough to whet its appetite, and bust their ass in a convincing way. Your pride and dignity has a higher priority and value than the foolishness of false friends. *You* are the predator in every section of the jungle you walk in! If you don't teach that to these people, you'll be in danger of forgetting it yourself, and that is entirely unacceptable!

It's unfortunate that your friends' knowledge of your martial art interest may bring out the worst in them. In many ways they're like the fools who poke a caged lion with a stick. *They come away with a sense of power by robbing you of yours.*

Is this acceptable to you—allowing social retards to stretch the ends of your patience and tolerance? If it is acceptable, I will tell you this—allow your beast to grow! Every day, in every way, in word, action, and deed, you teach people how you *will* be treated, which might be vastly different from how you *want* to be treated.

Think about that for a moment and let it soak in. The best way to teach acquaintances not to manhandle you is to confront them at the very first instance. When you become assertive enough to stand up for yourself with people who maul you, the beast within begins to grow. And when you believe in yourself enough to be willing to trash these people if they don't get the message, you'll own a bigger piece of the jungle! The inner beast won't let you down if you won't let it down.

Still, there is a delicate balance in what constitutes wholesome physical fun and what's considered horseplay. This has to be determined by you. A good yardstick to measure it by is how you think of yourself during or afterward. Are you exhilarated and happy or are you a little embarrassed and ashamed? If you can mix it up with your buddies and get bounced, jostled, or tossed into something and come away feeling good about it, then this doesn't apply to you. You have enough confidence in yourself to play without getting robbed in the process. But if you *don't* feel good about it, step aside and let them know you aren't a part of it. *Dare to be alone!*

Being a predator and living a large beast doesn't mean you have to stalk restlessly all about and look menacing. People who do this are more absorbed in the image they create than living the life of peace a predator should enjoy.

Look at predators in the wild. They generally live a peaceful and sleepy existence, occupying their time and days with scratching, yawning, napping, and roaming. It even appears as though at any time you could just walk right up and pet them; that is, until they get . . . *hungry*. Or you violate their space, person, or territory. Then you get a glimpse at the *nature* of the beast rather than the image, and *that* is a nightmare you won't want a part of!

Timing isn't everything, *it's the only thing!* I know, I know, you've heard that bromide before, and it was about winning. Still, as far as predation is concerned, it's more applicable to us as timing.

Since it's a given that we're going to get that ever-popular first shot in, it would make good sense to make the most of it. It's important in more ways than you might now realize. You know that strategically it's the right thing to do. You know psychologically it's the right thing to do. It's also physiologically the right thing to do.

Huh? What do I mean? Okay, look at it this way. If you say to someone, "C'mon, put 'em up. I'm gonna knock you on your ass!" he will more than likely knock *you on your ass* when you finish that sentence.

Still, let's say he's not too bright and says back to you, "Oh yeah!?" (a snappy comeback like that always gives them away), and then he puts up his dukes. Right off the starting gate, you hit him full in the face with a right punch, followed by a quick combination of punches and kicks. He's stunned and staggered as you press your attack, but he rallies his wits and wades through your attack to thoroughly beat the crap out of you.

Oh, I forgot to tell you, this was a *real big guy* I got you in a fight with. And while what you did stunned him, it didn't hurt him. And why wasn't he hurt? Even after you hit him with everything you had before he hit you, he still wasn't even close to being knocked out.

But there's more to timing than simply getting in the first strike. The time to strike is when he's least prepared. Short of popping

THAT GOLDEN MOMENT

him in the snout while he's coming out of the shower stall, you'll have to be attuned to the pace and tempo of the scenario you're directly involved in. Blast him within the time frame when he's either mid-sentence when speaking, getting ready to speak, getting out of a chair, or in any other space of time in which he's vulnerable.

Vulnerable. That's an important word to you, and you should keep it in mind when you're looking for your opportune "moment" to put him away.

In the above scenario where you struck the big guy first and hard, you still lost your edge because *he was prepared*. When someone is prepared to fight, there's a change in his attention and set of the musculature that allows him the physical ability to rock 'n roll with you. He can take a hard shot to the head and roll with it. And the only reason he can roll with it and still come after you is because he was prepared for that possibility.

Let's look at this issue in another way. Let's say you're going to water-ski off the end of a dock. Let's also say the handle to the ski rope is wrapped and tied to the palms of your hands and wrists so you're unable to let go. Since you've made a lot of starts from the dock, you're prepared for a certain measure of stress and pressure to your arms in order to hold onto the rope and land on your skis in the water when the boat roars away. It's tough, but you can do it. *You expect it. You've done it before.*

The boat's idling, and the driver told you he won't be ready for 10 more minutes. So you relax and let your mind wander for a moment. Suddenly the boat races away while you're daydreaming. Your arms are jerked out of their sockets as you're jerked out of your skis. The driver lied to you so you'd relax and wouldn't be prepared, and you weren't (that's right, he's a psycho). Because you were relaxed, *you became immediately vulnerable!*

So, the most opportune time for you to strike should be the least opportune time for your prey. And to that end, you should be prepared to say and do whatever you need to in order to gain that golden moment when your prey is least prepared for your sudden and violent attack.

There's such a wide range of circumstances you can find yourself involved in in a predator/prey encounter that it would take more time and space than is practical in a book to explore. Still, you can break the encounters down into two categories: immediate action and elapsed-time action.

Immediate action is as the name implies, in that you would act immediately if you were attacked. Elapsed-time action is a situation in which your prey makes his intentions known, and you have the latitude to assess and solve your situation with diplomacy or violence.

For instance, let's say you have a small traffic accident, a minor fender bender. It's a small accident for you because you're driving a real old beat-up car; the other guy is driving a new Corvette. (I know, I got you beat up at the start of this chapter, then your arms jerked out by a crazy boat driver, and now I have you driving a piece of crap car while the *other guy* gets the cool one. All this better be worth it!)

You get out of your car to exchange

license numbers and insurance information, and you're nervous and embarrassed. He gets out of his car in a rage. He's yelling at the top of his lungs, *and he tells you he's going to beat the hell out of you!* You can tell by the intensity of his anger that you're going to have a fight.

So, do you take up a boxing or karate stance and prepare to fight with him? Do you rush him before he gets to you and try to hit him first? Do you try to shout him down? Reason with him? Apologize profusely? Try to diffuse the situation with charm and humor? Think about this one for a few moments before you read any further.

I won't tell you precisely what to do, even though that may be why you bought this book. But I will tell you this: you can lose a fight, especially when the other guy is enraged and thoroughly motivated to liquify you, *regardless of your martial art experience!* What's my point? Don't fight him, *destroy* him!

The most expedient way to destroy large prey is to utilize to the best of your advantage that "golden moment" of vulnerability. To that end, you will have to be creative, if not downright theatric, about gaining that moment.

In the example above where your prey is getting out of his car, approaching you, and telling you that he intends you great bodily harm, *don't indicate to him that you agree to participate in your own destruction by assuming a fighting stance!*

Instead, consider holding your hands to your head to feign an injury. Stagger a bit if you think it'll help, or make motions with your hands as though you're deaf and trying to communicate with him. Or hold your hands up, palms out in supplication, giving him the impression you want to reason with him. Use any ploy that will take him aback, even for a brief shining second where confusion, doubt, or uncertainty registers on his face or in his actions.

In–that–moment—in the space of time between your last heartbeat and your next breath—explode into your attack! If your hands are up, you'll be in good position to launch an attack to support some powerful shin strikes to the sides of his legs above the knees, and you'll already be in position to ward off blows if you weren't quick enough to attack in the moment (figs. 130, 131, 132, 133).

A predator never betrays his intentions to his prey. Should you be in a situation where you're seeking out your prey for a specific reason, like for fondling your spouse or child, or for hurting someone you love in any way at all, and you find it necessary to hurt them, be casual.

For example, you're in a bar or at a party. You go to the rest room, and when you return your friend tells you she was groped by that big guy over there at the bar. Maybe you know him, maybe you don't. Regardless, don't act right away! He'll be watching you and expecting you to come after him. He'll be prepared. Instead, bide your time for a little while.

When you feel enough time has gone by, slowly stroll over to where he is. Take out some money from your wallet and sift through the bills as you approach him. Money always gets attention. In this in-stance, it will detract his attention from you. He expects you to come gunning for him

Figure 130

Figure 131

Figure 132

Figure 133

and it will confuse him to see you approaching with money in your hands and a smile on your face. In the confusion of the first seconds of what you say to him, mid-sentence, *put him down hard!*

I give this example only to illustrate my point about stalking your prey and taking it down. Don't use this as a guideline. You'll have to be creative in your own approach.

Devote some time and attention to what you might be able to do in the way of deception to get you close enough to your prey, in a vulnerable state of mind, to effect whatever kind of attack that feels most natural to you. If you're practiced in this and have a pretty good idea of just what you might do in a given situation, you'll be honing an important, if not primary, skill as a predator.

If you still feel uncomfortable about being a predator, you can look at it in another way. You can liken predation skills to self-preservation instincts enhanced to their ultimate peak. Predators are, by nature and definition, survivors. If you're willing to do whatever is necessary or distasteful to survive among dangerous prey, then you are a predator, whether you want to be called one or not.

Being human and communicating by spoken and written language, we're limited to rhetoric and semantics to describe what is indescribable. The empowering feeling of a beast unleashed to frighten, wound, or kill its prey is profound beyond words. The simple acknowledgment and calm acceptance of the existence of the beast within the heart of the predator is also a feeling beyond the reach of words.

Still, we have the capacity inherent within our species to be self-aware. And in order to become fully aware of who we really are, instead of the fantasies and delusions of who we'd like to think we are, we have to accept the many facets of our identities that we call our personalities, and also accept the duality of our nature to be both greedy and generous, honest and dishonest, coward and hero, predator and prey. In that acceptance, and in the practice of nurturing the beast, you'll find a place within yourself that is known and familiar even though you think you're just now learning of it.

I'm reiterating this point again this late in the book to remind you that you aren't necessarily learning something new insomuch as you're remembering something you forgot you knew. And to that end, you need to practice and devote yourself to training to be the best possible predator you're capable of in order to fully exploit that "golden moment" when it presents itself.

If you don't have the confidence to exploit the moment, *you won't recognize it when it occurs!* Please read this again because it is vitally important that you fully realize and accept the fact that it is *you,* and the beast *within you,* that will save your life by seizing the moment to pounce on your prey. It is *you,* and not a martial art style, that will save your life. All any martial art style can possibly be is a word for a way of possibilities.

It is your conscious decision to be either predator or prey. If you look to others for your strength, their beasts will consume your own, despite their good intentions, for that is the nature of a predator. When you nurture strength of spirit and take charge of your own life and the responsibility to protect it, your inner beast will come back to life and grow to prodigious proportions.

It is you that has mastery of the inner beast, and you that allows it to grow or die. Life is always larger when you're willing to take a large bite of it!